Motivating Hispanic Employees:

A Practical Guide to Understanding and Managing Hispanic Employees

D1056696

Carlos Conejo

What Others Have to Say about *Motivating Hispanic Employees*

"If you haven't noticed the 'Hispanic Worker Wave,' then you aren't noticing what is in your immediate future. Carlos Conejo provides a valuable service to employers by writing cogently and sensitively about aspects of Hispanic culture that affect performance in the workplace. If your company's profits depend on motivating Hispanic employees, read this book."

- Jim Tunney, former NFL Referee and co-author of *Chicken Soup for the Sports Fan's Soul*

"Carlos Conejo's material has helped us achieve new levels of multicultural understanding. Mastering this understanding has tangibly impacted our bottom line."

- Joe Burdow, President of Val-Pak Systems, Cox Target Media

"This is cutting-edge material that will change the way management looks at employee development."

– Ed Rigsbee, author of *Art of Partnering, Developing Strategic Alliances* and *PartnerShift*

"Carlos is a motivational speaker and trainer extraordinaire."

– Jesus Chavarria, editor and publisher of *Hispanic Business Magazine*

Motivating Hispanic Employees: A Practical Guide to Understanding and Managing Latino Employees

Published by Multicultural Press Publishing
Thousand Oaks, CA 91362
Phone: 805-494-0378   Fax: 805-494-8829
E-mail: carlos@mculture.net
Internet: www.mculture.net

Printed in the United States

Library of Congress Cataloging-in-Publication
7/1/2001

Conejo Carlos, A.
Motivating Hispanic Employees/Carlos
Conejo – 2nd Ed.
          p.cm.
ISBN 0-9706218-3-3

1. Management. 2. Business 2. Culture

Contents

About The Author

Carlos Conejo is a highly sought after management consultant on the rapidly-growing multicultural marketplace, he conducts major work internationally in the areas of workforce development, lean manufacturing, and marketing to emerging markets in either English, OR Spanish.

Additionally, he has been named one of the top U.S. Hispanic speakers by the independent firm of MarketData.

Mr. Conejo is a 1979 graduate of Pepperdine University, in Malibu, California, with a degree in Business Administration, and has held successful careers as Sales, Marketing and Product Manager in for almost 20 years. He has been trained in Lean enterprise, Effective Coaching, Behavioral Hiring and Firing, demographics, psychographics, Neurolinguistics, and Situational Leadership®. He has utilized this real-world experience to achieve tremendous success for both service and manufacturing organizations in effectively motivating, coaching and empowering hundreds of Hispanic employees to become more self-directed, self-reliant and more productive individuals.

Mr. Conejo has been lecturing and consulting internationally on management and supervision, coaching, and multicultural issues in Canada, Puerto Rico, and The United Kingdom, presenting to thousands of people from various organizations and companies including: International Bowling Industry, Cisco Brothers Fine Furniture (Their furniture featured on the set of Friends TV Show), Cox Target Media, Dun & Bradstreet, Greenlee-Textron, Hispanic Broadcasting Network, Hispanic Business Magazine, Good Nite Inns, Holiday Inn, Hilton, Hyatt, Sheraton Hotels, and other properties, KWHY TV-22 (#1 Independent Spanish-language television station in largest Spanish-speaking market- Los Angeles, CA), Firecraft Technologies-Lennox Industries, Meeting Professionals International (MPI), Professionals In Human Resources Association (PIHRA), Quality Chek'd Dairy Association, Silvercrest Western Homes - Division of Champion Homes, Small Business Administration's: Small Business Development Centers, State of California Manufacturing and Technology Centers, U.S. Department of Labor Region IX, U.S. Postal Service, U.S. Federal Executive Board, and more!

This book will show you how the transformational changes of Hispanic employees can be used as a competitive weapon for your organization in an ever-increasing global society.

Mr. Conejo is known as the Bilingual Dynamo ® and has been featured on the Lifetime Channel, KNBC-TV, and numerous other national television and radio shows. His bilingual audiocassette, 7 Secrets For Your Success/Siete Secretos Para Tu Exito is in its second edition. He is currently writing other multicultural books and curriculum.

For more information please contact Multicultural Associates

Tel: (805) 494-0378
Fax: (805) 494-8829

Carlos@mculture.net or
Info@mculture.net

Please visit Carlos Online at:

www.mculture.NET

Acknowledgements

They say that we all arrive on someone else's shoulders. I would like to thank God for all His provision. I still pray for discernment, patience and understanding.

I also would like to acknowledge my family for their love and support of my passion over the years. I know it was tough to give up corporate job security, but you hung in there with me. To my wife, for her love, encouragement and hard work. To my children for their encouragement and love. I never let those "pooh-pooh heads of doom" get me down! Thank you for putting up with my computer "pie eyes" when I work too long. Thank you for putting up with my grouchiness and the traveling. Look for continued excitement in our journey together.

Thank you to Jan and Audrey for believing in me and for your love and generosity.

Finally, this book would not be possible without the assistance of many individuals who have contributed to my success throughout the years.

My core buddies from Highland Park who have always been there for me: Nick Bernal, John Gay, Steve Hayashi and Roy Martinez. Thank you to those who listened, believed and molded me:
Dr. Juan Andrade, Jr., Chuck Blackburn, Carlos Escabosa, Larry and Kirk Dewitt, Victor Hand, Larry Ketchum, Harvey MacKay, Jim Pelley,

Dan Poynter, Peter Quan, Nido Qubein, Ed Rigsbee, Israel Rodriguez, Sr., Grady Reed and Jim Tunney, Ph.D.

Special thanks to Jerry Sanders, Mort Utley and Zig Ziglar. You guys changed my life!

Preface

- Have you tried to tap the Hispanic talent in your organization or company, but are unsure of the motives and values behind Hispanic employee behavior?
- What are Hispanic needs in the workplace and how can you, as an employer, satisfy them?
- Are there cultural differences between first and second generation Hispanics?

This book is designed for individuals and organizations that work with poorly-educated, low-skilled, Spanish-speaking, or Spanish dominant U.S. Hispanic employees or co-workers. Not all Hispanics lack formal education or require the type of training mentioned in this book, but 15 million of the current 35 million U.S. Hispanics do not have a high school degree. This book is designed for business owners, department heads, middle managers, and supervisors that work with these 15 million. This book is designed to give you practical ways to increase your awareness of Hispanic needs, cross the cultural gap, communicate more effectively and motivate these low-skilled Hispanic employees. You'll also learn to tap the mother lode of untapped talent to increase Hispanic employee participation, productivity and profitability.

This book will arm you with effective and practical solutions based on years of hands-on experience.

As an immigrant from Costa Rica, an employee and a manager, I've witnessed first-hand how Hispanic talent in the workplace is under-utilized and mis-managed. Using the solid scientific tools and management methods outlined in this book will allow you to create happier, more productive and self-reliant Hispanic employees.

Introduction

The term "Hispanic" refers to people who were born in (or whose families are from) Mexico, Spain or Latin America. The term "Latino" is synonymous with Hispanic. Often "Latino" is preferred west of the Mississippi in places like California and Texas, while "Hispanic" is more often heard in the east. I will use either term throughout this book.

Hispanics comes in all shapes, sizes and colors. For example, both Sammy Sosa (dark-skinned) and President Fujimori of Peru (light-skinned) are Latinos.

Hispanic is not a race, but a culture. Most Latinos are of a mixed race. Some are "mestizos" or descendents of Spaniards and indigenous Indians. Hispanics that have migrated from Mexico might be part Aztec or Maya. Many immigrants from Argentina will have ancestors from Germany, Britain and other European countries. There are a dozen major languages spoken in South America and another 2000 local or indigenous dialects. Hispanics are indeed a diverse group.

This book will deal with these immigrants and subsequent generations that have made their lives in America and sought greater opportunity and better lives for them and their families. These new "Americans" are increasingly hired by public and private organizations for their strong work ethic and loyalty. In many cases, Latinos are hired without having any knowledge of English. Some organizations seek out Hispanic employees for their stamina and work ethic. Others hire Hispanics with an eye toward exploitation knowing that Hispanics (or other recent immigrants) will work hard to "get a foot up in this world" to provide for their families.

This book will provide you with practical management tools to help you eliminate conflict address potential language barriers and avoid misunderstandings with your Hispanic employees. These tools will foster more effective communication, create higher morale, greater teamwork and increased productivity.

Chapter 1

The "Hispanization" of America

Population growth

There are more than 35 million Hispanics living in the United States, representing roughly 13 percent of the nation's population. By the year 2050, Hispanics will number 96 million people, comprising 24 percent of the population.

U.S. Hispanic Population 1990 to 2025

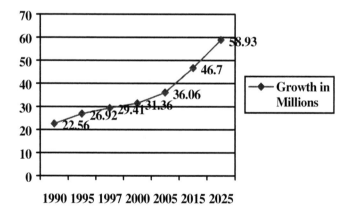

Source: U.S. Census

The chart below illustrates the growth of the Hispanic population relative to the mainstream population (non-Hispanic whites) for the period 1970-1990. The mainstream population grew 24 percent during this period, while the Hispanic population increased at a rate of 253 percent.

20 Year Growth Rates 1970-1990

Source: U.S. Census

The conclusion from this is simple: Hispanic families are having more babies. Latino families average four children per household, whereas non-Hispanic whites average 2.3 children per household.

The Hispanic market has the fastest-growing middle class growth. Last year, Hispanics bought 70 percent of homes purchased in Los Angeles County.

The number of Latino-owned business has increased more than 700 percent in the past 25 years. Latinos make up a significant percentage of our nation's workforce.

Purchasing power

The Hispanic or Latino population in the U.S. currently has a purchasing power of more than $500 billion. This number is expected to jump to $1 trillion dollars within ten years, making Hispanics an attractive target group.

The discretionary income of Hispanics has almost doubled in the past decade to total $72 million.

The number of Latino middle class households (those with more than $40,000 in annual income) increased from just fewer than 1.5 million in 1979 to nearly 2.7 million in 1998. This represents an 80 percent increase in just 20 years. The percentage of each subgroup that has reached middle class incomes is as follows:

U.S.-born Cuban	63%
U.S.-born Mexican	41%
U.S. mainland-born Puerto Ricans	38%
Other U.S.-born Hispanics	46%

The Charts below illustrate the steady growth of U.S. Latino incomes between 1979 and 1998. The charts compare the difference in income between U.S. born Hispanics and foreign-born Hispanics. The higher U.S.-born incomes are due to the attainment of higher education, against the shear numbers of uneducated or under-educated immigrants entering this country.

Income All Latino Households

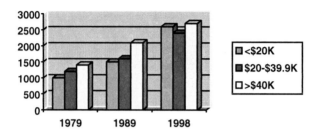

Income U.S. Hispanics

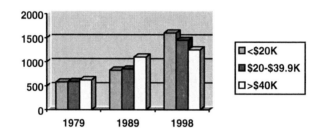

Foreign-Born Hispanic Income

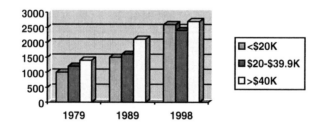

Source: Tomás Rivera Policy Institute

These charts illustrate the importance of educating both U.S.-born and immigrant Hispanics to the point where they can realize their education and income potential. Both of these factors become critical to the future vibrancy and economic development of the U.S. economy. Additionally, as our nation experiences "Hispanization", as an employer, you need to prepare your organization's future leaders, many of whom will be, or are already Hispanic.

Segmentation

Segmentation of Hispanics varies from state to state and from region to region. On the west coast, Mexicans, Central American and South Americans are the largest groups of Hispanics. More than half of these (65 percent) are of Mexican descent.

In the Midwest, the Mexican population is in its fourth generation. Thirty-five percent of Chicago is of Mexican descent.

On the East Coast, cities like Orlando and Miami have large Cuban and Puerto Rican populations. A large number of Puerto Ricans have also settled in New York, New Jersey and Connecticut.

Hispanics are also widely found in cities and states not traditionally considered "Hispanic," such as Atlanta (GA), Madison (WI), Iowa, Kansas and Arkansas.

Hispanic diversity

Hispanics are the fastest growing minority group in America, but they are not a homogenous community. The U.S. Census estimates 65 percent of Hispanics are of Mexican origin. Mexican-Americans have the lowest educational level among Hispanics.

Approximately 12 percent of U.S. Hispanics are from Puerto Rico and another six percent from Central America. The majority of immigrants from Central America come from El Salvador (50 percent), Guatemala (20 percent) and Nicaragua (15 percent). Only five percent of Hispanics come from South America, the majority from Colombia, Ecuador, Peru, Argentina and Chile. Five percent of U.S. Hispanics come from Cuba and another four percent are from Spain.

Extended families – "Collective Society"

Hispanics come from a collective society. The entire community is generally of greater importance than is the individual. *La familia es todo* (Family is everything) is an honorable concept, but caries many responsibilities and burdens. Some Hispanics must work to support their household and extended family, which may include cousins or nephews who share the same house. Some Hispanics must leave school to work or become caregivers.

Assimilation or acculturation

There are several levels of assimilation for U.S. Hispanics:

- Recent immigrants: Relate culturally to their homelands
- First generation: Understand parents' sacrifices; may be bicultural
- Second and consecutive generations: Middle class values; have lower incomes and lower education levels
- Pioneers: Mexican families that were either here when the sunbelt states were still part of Mexico or arrived with the initial Spanish exploration

Nationalism

The United States is often referred to as a "melting pot" of peoples, cultures and communities. Immigrants have come to the U.S. for generations and blended together to create the American fabric. The Hispanic community, however, is more like a "salad" than a melting pot. In the same bowl you have *pepinos* (cucumbers) who don't want to work with the *tomates* (tomatoes). The *lechuga* (lettuce) dislikes the *olivas* (olives). There are Mexicans, Central Americans and Argentines. One is more Indian, while another is more "pure-bred."

How does this translate into the workplace? Nationalism among Latinos' diverse groups can lead to conflict, loss of productivity, lower quality work and miscommunication. As a manager of Latino workers, you should recognize that nationalistic pride is a motivating dynamic and must be effectively handled to properly motivate Hispanic and Spanish-speaking employees.

Respect and deference

There is a prevalent hierarchy or pecking order within the Hispanic community:

1. Elders
2. Parents
3. Priest
4. Teacher
5. Academia
6. Politician
7. Businessperson

This can be beneficial when older or experienced individuals are considered mentors. The hierarchy can also be limiting, particularly when the elders in the community have little or no formal education. In a business setting, there's also the danger that these individuals will insist on absolute homage or control, refusing to share leadership and resisting change. I call this "burro management."

Education

Education is a very big subject within the Hispanic community, but the graduation attainment has not kept up with reality due to various reasons. The following chart compares the education level attained by U.S. Hispanics and non-Hispanic whites:

	U.S. Hispanics	Non-Hispanic Whites
Less than high school	43.9%	4.5%
High school diploma	26.9	34.3
Associate's degree	18.4	25.7
Bachelor's degree	7.8	18.5
Master's degree	3.1	9.1
Doctorate degree	2.3	7.9

On average, U.S.-born Hispanics have 2-3 years more schooling and 30 percent higher wages than do recent immigrants. However, U.S.-born Cubans and Central/South Americans meet or exceed the education levels of non-Hispanic whites.

According to the Tomás Rivera Policy Institute, the percentage of native-born Hispanics with a college education rose from 10.7 in 1979 to 15.4 in 1998, an increase of 43.9 percent.

Approximately 44 percent of Mexican-Americans have earned a high school diploma and another 6 percent have college degrees. While education is considered important and stressed publicly, family (*la familia*) is a higher priority. Older children are expected to support the family, even if that means dropping out of school to do so.

Hispanic population by occupation

Between 1990 and 1996, the number of Hispanics with management and professional positions increased nearly 49 percent, although Hispanics make up only 19 percent of the total number of managers and professionals, as seen below:

Percentage of U.S. Hispanic Population by Occupation	
Managerial	12.1%
Professional	6.8%
Technical	2.4%
Administrative Support/Clerical	9.3%
Sales	9.0%
Private Household Services	0.1%
Protection Services	0.8%
Other Services	6.7%
Farming/Forestry/Fishing	5.1%
Precision Production/Craft/Repair	13.7%
Machine Operators	24.0%
Transportation/Material Moving	5.6%
Handlers/Equipment	4.4%
Total	100.0%

Chapter 2

Values, Needs and Expectations of the Hispanic Employee

The work ethic is an extremely important value in the Hispanic community. It is considered an honor to have work. Sweat is often a measure of honest work, and a man is judged by how hard he works. It is a disgrace to be called *flojo* (lazy) or to ask for assistance. Hispanics are generally grateful for their jobs.

Virtuous, isn't it? To an extent, yes, but let's look at how these values can affect your organization.

This deep-rooted value to work hard may prevent Hispanic employees from carrying out their workload in an efficient and effective manner. They might be very task-oriented, and pay little attention to results. In their effort to work hard, they might not be working smart. Quality might be suffering. This can be detrimental to you and your clients, particularly if you have not shown your employees what quality results look like.

Pride and loyalty

In addition to a strong work ethic, Hispanic employees are also proud and loyal workers. When channeled in the right direction, pride can be beneficial. It can be detrimental, however, when it causes a lack of initiative, poor quality or poor communication.

Hispanics are fiercely loyal to their language and culture. Many prefer to speak Spanish, even after living in the U.S. for years. Often companies do not encourage communication in English and don't offer Vocational English as a Second Language classes (VESL). Although employers should encourage English, they should also provide the tools to learn it.

Cultural differences

The following chart summarizes key values and cultural differences between Hispanics and the mainstream American culture:

Americans	Hispanics
View of time	
Precious commodity not to be wasted; multi-tasking common; time is money	Precious commodity to be enjoyed, not rushed; time is flexible

Culture

Competitive; individual is more important than the group	Collective; cooperation; decisions are group-oriented

View of money

Something to possess; bottom line profit focus in the workplace	Status symbol; offers security and respect

View of God

God will provide; "give me" Lord	God willing... (it's out of my Hands; fatalistic mentality)

Lucky number

7	8

Unlucky number

13	7

Colors

Red, white, blue (patriotic) Black (death, formal)	Yellow (lucky) Purple (unlucky, death)

Eye contact

Looking someone in the eye when speaking is a sign of honesty and respect	Mexicans and some Central Americans look down/away to show respect* South Americans tend to look at you straight in the eye, but it is rude to stare or gawk.

Body language

Less "touchy," fewer gestures	More touchy, more gestures

Personal space

More important Don't crowd me...	Less important Touching while sitting close is OK

Classroom or meeting situation

Order, restraint, respect for the Speaker. One listens forms opinions. Singular learning	Everyone speaks at once. Unofficial groups form to discuss opinions Consultative Learning

Men-Women Relationships

When it comes to viewing women, Mexicans and Central Americans commonly stare, gawk and wolf-call as accepted behavior. To minimize this behavior in the workplace, female managers should be careful not to wear clothing with short hemlines or low necklines. Additionally, you may want to provide Preventing Sexual Harassment or Diversity classes which address alternative lifestyles to educate on American customs and proper workplace conduct, familiarity

Hispanics are very "touchy" and expressive with their body language among family and friends. Often Hispanics talk at once and very loudly. Gestures may be very broad or large. This can be disconcerting, especially in a business meeting. Don't get frustrated, just redirect the participant's back to the subject at hand, and ask questions. You may also want to observe the grouping that has emerged and ask each group for feedback. This is the Latino way of synthesizing information.

Watch where you touch a Hispanic employee, as it may be interpreted as demeaning, discriminatory or patronizing. Never pat anyone on the head! Here are some basic guidelines when it comes to appropriate touch:

- You may touch the shoulders, but not the arms around the shoulders
- Shaking hands with either one or both hands is normal. When shaking with both, your hands clasp both sides of the person's hand. Try learning the Hispanic handshake of choice at your facility. It's usually a three or four step handshake. Let the Hispanic person lead you through this ritual; don't initiate it on your own unless you are readily familiar with the person.
- You may lightly touch the forearm or upper arm, as when making a point or to get their attention.

I would recommend refraining from hugs and embraces in the workplace with an employee of either gender. You can get to know Hispanic employees by hosting a pot luck dinner. Break bread with the entire group. This way you won't be offending anyone by showing favoritism. Hugs and embraces may be appropriate outside the workplace, but always follow their cue.

It is considered bad manners to slouch, lean or plop into your chair. It is also bad manners to walk into a room when others are present without acknowledging everyone's presence by looking around while greeting (to catch everyone's eye if possible). Even functionally illiterate Hispanic employees practice this formal etiquette. Some Hispanic cultures require that you say shake hands as you say goodbye to everyone in the group before exiting a room or meeting. Follow their cue.

Hispanics may not keep appointments as precisely as you may be used to. Hispanics often arrive late. This may be a sign of respect for the host. There is also the philosophy of *mañana*, which literally means "tomorrow." Since the future is not definite, one should savor the moment and put other things off until tomorrow. When I was a child, my parents would always say, *Si Dios quiere, llegamos a mañana*, (If God wants us to be here tomorrow, we will be.) and *¿Quién sabe si llegamos a mañana?* (...if we make it until tomorrow). It still drives me nuts when my parents say this, because of its fatalistic mentality. Employers should explain the importance of deadlines from the customer's perspective. Help Hispanics adapt to the sense-of-urgency to compete in today's face-paced environment (what Bill Gates calls "business at the speed of thought").

Eye contact does not have the same effect in all cultures. In America, steady eye contact indicates honesty and sincere interest in the other party. We expect people to look us in the eye; otherwise we are suspicious and tend not to trust the other person.

In some Hispanic cultures, averting your eyes or looking down is a sign of respect. However, most of the educated, assimilated Hispanic men prefer direct eye contact and dealing *cara a cara* (face to face).

How do all of these Hispanic needs and values play out in the workforce? Here are some real-life examples from my experience.

EXAMPLE ONE

Failure to understand cultural differences regarding eye contact can have devastating effects. A para-educator who had been with the school district more than ten years suddenly slammed her hand on the desk of a Hispanic high school student who was in a special education class. She then shouted, "Look at me when I am talking to you!" Talk about raising a huge barrier! The poor kid had been doodling, which told me he was a kinesthetic learner and didn't need to watch the teacher in order to process the information. You can bet the teacher and I had a little enlightenment talk after that.

EXAMPLE TWO

At the beginning of my speaking career, I conducted seminars for Dun & Bradstreet Business Education Services. They booked me for a night in a luxury hotel in Boulder, Colorado. The hotel brochure boasted of its "impeccable amenities."

I entered my "impeccable" room only to find chipping paint on the bathroom door frame, a deteriorating toilet seat, a broken chair, a filthy ice bucket and stains on the chair pillow. For all intents and purposes, the room had been "cleaned." It had been vacuumed; the sheets had hopefully been changed, etc. To make a long story short: Housekeeping had "cleaned" this room. This was the task. Apparently, no one had bothered to tell the housekeeper that she must report all potential maintenance issues that might affect a guest's stay. I requested that I change rooms, only to find the second room less "impeccable" than the first. I spoke with the manager and she acknowledged that the hotel had training issues with the housekeeping staff, which was predominantly Hispanic.

Are there similarities between the Hispanic employees in these examples and those of your organization? Do your employees jump to complete their assigned task, but very narrowly? Do they finish the task quickly, failing to ask questions and then proceed to make many mistakes?

Set objective standards of excellence

Make sure your employees know what the standards are and how they will be measured. Rather than rely on job descriptions, create activity and task descriptions so employees understand the entire scope of their responsibilities. Explain what minimum standards you are willing to tolerate, what you consider a good or competent job, and what you consider an excellent job. By providing clearly defined guidelines and objectives you are allowing the Hispanic employee a range of performance standards that they can measure up to. This will increase the Hispanic employee's awareness and productivity. Many Hispanic employees come from extremely modest backgrounds and tend to "make due," which often explains why they will tolerate deplorable working conditions. It is up to you, the employer, to set clear standards and clearly communicate them to your employees.

Consider having your employees devise their own mission and vision statements for their particular areas of responsibility. This creates pride and accountability. The concept of vision and mission, however, will be foreign to most Hispanic employees. Invest time in familiarizing them with these concepts. You can tie this in to creating a vision and mission statement for their home life and their children. (Remember, family is the first priority for Latinos.)

If you have Hispanic employees that are recent immigrants, ask them about their journey to the United States. Why did they come to the U.S.? The answer will most likely be "to create a better life" or "to have more opportunity." Explain how these are the same reasons you want them to formulate a mission and vision statement for their work. Drawing a parallel between their family life and their work one will enable greater understanding. Since Hispanics are a highly social and collective group, have a weekly meeting, at least, with Hispanic employees in your organization. Show them what you want them to do and explain the company's standards of quality.

- EXPLAIN what you want your Hispanic employees to do.
- SHOW them what you want done.
- Allow them to PRACTICE the task. Offer immediate suggestions, make corrections and clearly communicate to avoid mistakes later.
- Solicit FEEDBACK that involves more than one of the senses (i.e. vision, smell, taste, and hearing). Everyone has a different learning style. Most Latino employees are "visual learners," meaning they learn best when seeing pictures or written instructions. "Auditory learners" prefer oral instructions. In soliciting feedback, incorporate more than one sense into your questions, for example:
  o Do you <u>see</u> what I am talking about? (visual)
  o What did you <u>think</u> about doing it that way? (auditory)
  o How did doing that <u>feel</u> to you? (kinesthetic)

This type of questioning will encourage dialogue and help you assess your employees' level of understanding. It will increase trust because your employees will feel that you are taking time to help them. If there are questions or doubts, you can address them immediately.

Questions involving multiple senses are important for other reasons as well. Most Latin American and Asian countries have "high context" cultures. These cultures rely more on pictures and nuances to convey meaning, rather than on the semantics of the words themselves. Chinese writing, for example, is made of combinations of symbols (as opposed to an alphabet of letters). One symbol or word can have a variety of meanings depending on the way it is said. In contrast, North Americans, the British, the Germans and the Swiss are considered "low context" communicators in that they rely on the words themselves.

As a result, employers would do well to have picture signs around the workplace in addition to signs having only words.

Monitor for consistent and continuous improvement

Don't rely on people to independently follow through unless they have a proven track record of self-reliance and reliability. Hispanic employees are reluctant to follow up because they don't want to be perceived as acting outside their scope of authority. Formally review employees at least once a quarter rather than annually. See chapter four for sample review forms.

In training team leaders for Lennox Industries in south central Los Angeles, for example, I discovered that the team leaders had little formal training in supervision and leadership skills. They were afraid to make decisions, fearing retribution from their supervisors and from other departments within the organization. This fear is a common one among Hispanic employees.

They are afraid the "master" will fire them for making independent decisions and suggestions. They are not used to working collaboratively with other departments. They don't know what process to follow to affect positive change. This knowledge gap can lead to finger-pointing, resentment and accusations of discrimination and even racism. It usually takes me 7-10 weeks of training to help Hispanics realize that this is not the case.

Because team leaders had not participated in formal training before, there was not only anticipation and excitement about the training, but some trepidation as well. The team leaders did not fully trust management's intentions. Management should clearly articulate the desired behavioral outcomes of the training and support the results of the training. It might be worth designating a "champion" at the executive level to make sure the changes are implemented throughout the organization and are linked with the company's goals and objectives. It's important to let the Hispanic employees know that this "champion" exists to assist them. This is very comforting and will pay great dividends in their development.

Conduct ongoing training

Some organizations have a continuous improvement training structure. Others conduct training on an "as needed" basis. Successful companies have ongoing training programs, which serve as great motivating factors for Hispanic employees.

Several years ago, I was training a company's gardening staff. The very first question these Hispanic employees asked was "what have we done wrong?" They thought the three-day training session was some sort of retaliatory move on the part of management. It was evident that management had not included these Hispanic employees in the training's planning stages.

When communicating the benefits of training to your employees, stress how the training will change both their work life and family life. Teach the Japanese method of *Kaizen*. "Kai" means "change" and "Zen" means "good." Together they mean "improvement."

Total Quality Management (TQM) is another approach worth adopting. With TQM, organizations strive to constantly improve every process and product by progressive methods. Both *Kaizen* and TQM should serve as the fabric of your organization's structure.

Provide training materials, signage and job aids in both English and Spanish. One company I worked with created a bilingual terminology notebook with words specific to their business. The employees identified this need and were able to complete the notebook in about four weeks. The notebook is now hanging from each machine in the company, serving as a valuable tool for English- and Spanish-speakers alike.

Teach meeting protocol

During meetings, encourage participation and questions. Allow only one person to speak at a time. The Japanese applaud each other as a means of rewarding and encouraging more participation. I have tried this method with Hispanic employees and they have responded favorably. Don't always be the one that calls or conducts the meeting. Rotate this responsibility. Assign a timekeeper if appropriate. Once everyone understands the ground rules, you'll begin to have more effective meetings. At first, you will encounter some resistance, but it's a cultural resistance based on group processing rather than resistance to comply. Be patient and be prepared to keep the training wheels on for as long as it takes for you to see some progress.

Build relationships

Employers should learn to understand the collective consciousness of Hispanic employees and take steps to build deeper and stronger relationships with them.

In the U.S., we can do business with someone without first establishing a personal relationship with that person. Power lunches are a common practice. Hispanics, however, are relationship-oriented and prefer to establish a solid foundation BEFORE doing business. Business is traditionally done away from the lunch or dinner table. It is considered rude to discuss business during a meal, since the needs of the people are placed above the "deal."

Problems and opportunities

In order to effectively motivate your Hispanic employees, you should first become familiar with common problems that might that they may face. The following chart identifies key issues and concerns that might apply to your workplace:

Issues & Concerns	Opportunities
Team Leader Literacy in English & Spanish	Train in Vocational English as a Second language (VESL)
Lack of Team Leader Experience/Exposure to Formal Training	Assess level of knowledge. Implement basic & intermediate supervisory & organizational development skills. Train-the-trainer.
Absence of team-Oriented Work	Build productive work teams and intradepartmental communications. Have employees create personal mission and vision statements that tie into the enterprise goals

	& objectives.
Idiosyncratic Supervisory Skills Idiosyncratic Supervisory Skills	Build consensus and similar "skill sets". Teach Team Stages: Forming, Storming, Norming, Conforming & Performing. Tie management styles to Enterprise mission and vision and goals and objectives.
Lack of Consistent Measurement & Reward System	Change written job descriptions to task & activity profiles spring boarding on "best practices." Measure quarterly skill sets: deficient, competent, and proficient levels of performance. Tie into reward system. Percentage or monetary bonus system: team rewards work best to get people collaborating. Tie everyone on the team to a minimum before payout. This gets peer pressure working for you. Generate Quarterly Employee Action Plans and measure against enterprise goals & Objectives. Provide objective measurement

	mechanism with daily tracking system.
Decision-making, Delegation & Authority Ambivalence	Provide participants with basic decision-making, 6-step problem solving model: Teach and practice force field, root cause, and cause & effect and fishbone analysis. (YES! Believe it. The trick is using lots of visuals to teach these concepts). Provide clear lines of authority and clear parameters. Reinforce this empowerment constantly.
Employee Satisfaction & Conflict	Build skills that enable effective communications, teach and measure personality styles, diversity and multicultural and lifestyle sensitivity. (Make the personality styles entertaining. Stay away from dry humor or dry instructors) Include all levels in 360-Degree evaluations then begin doing something immediately to remove "barriers" in the system!
Dedicated & full-time	It's a good idea to have

Human Resources Manager/trainer. Ideally, bilingual and bicultural would be a definite plus! Hire for solid people skills & knowledge and sense-of-urgency. Last thing you need is a bureaucrat in this position. Let attorney handle compliance issues. an on-site "champion" that will help in taking your organization to the next level of excellence. Hispanic employees want someone that will be their advocate until they learn how to be fully empowered. Hire for Kaikaku (radical change) in human relations and productivity. This is a must in order for your organization to compete globally!

Organizational Readiness and Barriers to Training:

Because many Hispanics may not have participated in formal training before. So you may find there is some anticipation and excitement about the training, but also some trepidation. I've entered sessions where the Hispanic employees thought that training had commenced as a punishment for bad behavior. Again the issue of Hispanic's trusting management's intentions is monumental. So I suggest that you involve Hispanic employees in the decision-making and planning early on. Make sure that management knows and articulates the desired behavioral outcomes and is committed to supporting the changes that result directly from the training. ALL management MUST be on board. There's nothing worse than trying to initiate change in your organization's Hispanic population only to have it sabotaged by management. In fact, you may want to implement a parallel management or executive coaching track simultaneously to the workforce track especially if your organization has managers whom may have seniority, but lack effective management and supervisory skills. I find a higher resistance to change in privately held companies. You may want to designate a management "champion" at the executive level to drive the new changes to the highest management levels and tie them into the enterprise goals and objectives. If privately held, make sure the principals are fully committed!

One excuse that you'll hear is that the organization will suffer due to time off afforded to attend class. Obviously, it would be nice to attend class after hours, but that may not always be possible. Sell the value and teach Hispanic employees how to delegate or "cover' while attending classes. After a few short weeks, everyone will be amazed that the place didn't fall apart while people are attending class. Sick to your class schedule classes, when mistakes happen. Otherwise this event becomes a scapegoat, another excuse to suspend the classes. Stay committed.

Previous Training Effectiveness:

Some organizations have a continuous training structure, or culture. Others are piecemeal or on an "as needed" basis. It's critical to your organization's well being that you gain Hispanic employees understanding and commitment as a continuous learning organization. When you reinforce it and include the Hispanic employees from the beginning and you allow them to discover their potential then you avoid the flavor-of-the-month mentality. This raises the level of trust and helps people deal with the constant change that has become part of today's business fabric. When you instill this in your employees, but especially Hispanic employees it becomes a great motivator.

Additionally it makes your organization more agile and nimble. I remember one organization where I was training their gardeners. On the first day of training the first question Hispanic employees asked was, "what have we done wrong?" They thought the upcoming three-day sessions were management's retaliation to something they had done wrong. It was very evident that management had not included any Hispanic employees in the planning stages or utilized "unofficial leaders" (elders or those with seniority) to communicate a positive message to the rest of the Hispanic employees.

Motivator:

Stress how the training received on the job will positively affect their work and home lives ("family.") Teach the Japanese method of Kaizen. Kai means, Change, Zen means good. Together they mean constant improvement. What this means is that once a change has been implemented, we search for the next improvement, and the next and the next. Instill this concept of continuous improvement into Hispanic employees so they will not perceive constant change as a negative, or management not knowing what they are doing.

Opportunities

Train in Vocational English as a Second Language (VESL).

Assess the level of knowledge. I use a simple math test to determine the level of education Spanish-speaking employees have attained. This is useful because math is a universal language. This assessment is 15 simple mathematical problems. I start off with simple addition and subtraction, followed by multiplication and long division. This is followed by simple fifth grade fractions. If the employee can complete 80-90% of the problems then they probably have a sixth to eight-grade education. If they cannot get past the long division, then they have less than a sixth grade education. If they are unable to complete any of the math, then I know I have a functionally illiterate employee on my hands.

Implement basic and intermediate supervisory/organizational development skills. Train the trainer to maximize the return on your investment...

Build productive work teams and intradepartmental communications. Have employees create personal mission and vision statements that tie into the goals and objectives of the organization.

Build consensus and similar "skill sets." Teach team stages: forming, storming, norming, conforming and performing. Tie management styles to the organizations' mission, vision, goals and objectives. Sensitize management to Hispanic needs: cultural and collective.

Change written job descriptions to task and activity profiles. Measure quarterly skill sets as deficient, competent or proficient. Tie into a reward system. Create rewards that foster family not competitiveness. Generate quarterly employee's action plans and measure against the company's goals. Provide objective management mechanism with daily tracking system.

Provide participants with basic decision-making, six-step problem solving model: force field, root cause, and cause & effect and fishbone analysis. Provide clear lines of authority.

Build skills that enable effective communication, diversity and multicultural sensitivity. Measure personality styles. Include all levels in 360-degree evaluation and begin removing "barriers" from the system.

Have an onsite "champion" to help take your organization to the next level of excellence. Hire for radical change in human relations and productivity. This is a must in order for your organization to compete globally.

The language barrier

This is a complicated issue based on the varying assimilation levels of U.S. Hispanics. I have provided below a table to give you a better sense of the different levels of assimilation for Hispanics. This table illustrates the general norm and may not hold true for some Hispanics in your organization.

Language and Cultural Preference

Status	Primary Language	Language Capability	Preferred Language at work	Preferred Language at Home	Cultural Affinity
Recent Immigrant	Spanish	Spanish	Spanish	Spanish	Hispanic
In U.S. 3-5 years	Spanish	Beginning Bilingual	Spanish	Spanish	Hispanic
In U.S. 5-10 years	Spanish	Functionally Bilingual	Spanglish	Spanglish #	Bicultural
In U.S. 10-20 years OR 2nd & 3rd Generation	English	Limited Bilingual	English	English Or Spanglish	Bicultural
U.S.- Born* 3rd + Generation	English	English	English	English	American

* Third- and fourth-generation Hispanics generally grow up with little or no Spanish spoken at home. As children, they adopt the norms and values of their local community, be it rural Mississippi or suburban Chicago.

Spanglish is slang – a combination of Spanish and English. People might say "marketa" for "market instead of the correct Spanish word, *mercado*. "Parquiar" and "parqueo" are other examples of Spanglish for "to park." The correct Spanish words are *estacionar* or *estacionamento*.

Chapter 3

The Quest for Empowerment

My primary intent is to help develop the Hispanic employees in your organization. My other intent is for my Hispanic colleagues and the Hispanic community to say, with a sigh of relief, "*Gracias a Dios* (Thank God), someone has articulated our needs, hopes and dreams."

As Zig Ziglar says: If there is hope in the future, there's power in the present. I want to help you empower my community so that everyone benefits. Here's how:

Tap into the leadership that exists within your organization.

When I conducted a 20-week Total Quality Management (TQM) curriculum at Firecraft Technologies, I learned that the average education level of the foremen was fourth grade. The foremen were asked to supervise 20 other employees, without having had formal supervisory training or related skills. They were also required to complete paperwork, handle calculations and read blueprints and other diagrams.

Many of these foremen stepped up to the plate over time and did a marvelous job in these technical tasks. What many of them lacked was the ability to lead and motivate others. Most had been operating out of instinct.

Recognize cultural barriers that may prevent Hispanics from succeeding

Entitlement

Hispanics often emigrate from countries that have socialistic infrastructures, such as socialized medicine and government-owned utilities. Many Hispanics feel that the "system" owes them something. Unfortunately, some organizations in the U.S. continue to perpetuate this sentiment by fostering a culture of dependency. Although there are plenty of worthwhile organizations and programs, I feel more organizations need to stress that all of us have the power to go after something and make it happen.

Fatalistic mentality

Since many decisions Hispanics make are based on their strong belief in God, the idea of personal accountability is less prevalent. Many Hispanics often say *Si Dios quiere* (if God wants or wills it for me, it's out of my hands). This fatalistic mentality can be detrimental in many areas, but especially in the workplace where taking responsibility and initiative need to be encouraged.

One way around this is to explain to your Hispanic employees how they can see direct results from taking the initiative, setting goals and welcoming responsibility. Try to tie in relevant examples from their home or family life. When speaking about goal-setting and meeting deadlines, for example, you might want to give an example of buying a home. In order to come up with the down payment, most families need to set specific financial goals. Once they make an offer on a home, the current owner has a deadline for responding to the offer. Since home ownership is of tremendous value to Hispanics, it is appropriate to use home-related examples to illustrate work-related concepts and tasks.

Family ties

There is often pressure to remain within the Hispanic community. Hispanics feel obligated to their heritage and community. A few years ago I spoke with a small merchant in Oxnard, CA. He forbade his oldest daughter to attend college because she was the eldest and a woman. Her obligation was to stay at home and run the family business. Even though several major colleges and universities were courting her, her father didn't budge. Wasn't the local community college good enough for her? This way she would be close to home and could help out with the business. He finally gave in only after the teachers and counselors from her high school convinced him to let her go to college.

Subservience

The effects of the Spanish conquistadors and subsequent wars are still being felt throughout Mexico and Latin America. When shaking hands with a Latino, he or she will often say *a sus órdenes*, meaning "at your service." In Mexico, people say *¿mande?* or "as you command; send me master," when they want someone to repeat what was said. In contrast, the English equivalent is simply "Pardon?" "What?" or "Would you mind repeating that?"

Hispanic employees might rush to do something you ask, without questioning it, rather than consider the best method for completing the task. They might be in such a rush to please you, the master, that it never occurred to them to stop and analyze all alternatives. This can cost your organization time and money in mistakes and poor quality.

<u>Sense of inadequacy or insecurity</u>

As children, Hispanics are often taught not to mix outside of their community. The *Americanos* are perceived as people who deserve respect and are somehow more intelligent, clever and business savvy. The American culture is very opportunity- and prosperity-driven, whereas Hispanics tend to be grateful for whatever they might have since it is God's will.

In a work setting, Hispanics might maintain their distance from Americans due to the Hispanics' sense of inadequacy, insecurity or due to the language barrier. This discomfort may cause your employees to remain quiet as a show of respect.

Discrimination

Sometimes discrimination is direct and other times it is subtler. I grew up in the inner city of Los Angeles. I attended a junior high school where there were fights by gangs EVERY DAY during lunch. Hispanics beating up other Hispanics. I could never figure this out. Why were kids from the same race always fighting?

I was beat up in the first grade and again in sixth grade. In high school, four friends and I were also "jumped" by a Hispanic gang. We were lucky to escape with our lives!

The ugly part of my community is that some of us get into pity parties of *pobresito* or "poor me, I'm being discriminated against," when many times we are dishing out more discrimination than we receive.

Hispanics are a diverse bunch. Sometimes disenfranchised, the Mexicans often hate the Puerto Ricans, the Puerto Ricans often hate the Mexicans, and the Central American countries often hate each other. So if you have a racially mixed workplace, even if it's 100 percent Hispanic, you are sure to have conflict!

To overcome this nationalistic sub-segmentation you need to create a nurturing environment of tolerance, of mutual respect and unity. Actively get Hispanic employees involved in concentrating on similarities and mutual objectives. One solution might be to create task teams made up of people from different Hispanic groups, which forces them to work together toward a common goal.

Train employees on personality styles, team stages and consensus BEFORE you create the task teams. Gain commitment toward "sensitivity issues" such as cultural differences, sexual harassment and alternate lifestyles. This commitment should come from all levels of management. Measure progress towards goals every three months.

Teach assertiveness, problem solving and team dynamics that deal with handling conflict in a positive manner. Help Hispanic employees understand that conflict is a normal part of the workplace, but help them differentiate between positive conflict: which creates innovation, and improves the process and destructive conflict: which creates gossip,
a hostile work environment, or poor quality. Provide a way or procedure for dealing with conflict, such as a short but formal grievance and appeals, or peer counseling and mentoring. Help your Hispanic employees understand that it's appropriate to question your ways. In fact, ask them to give you two ways they can improve the work they're doing right now. Then guide them in implementing their ideas. The more reinforcement they receive from you the more they will trust and believe you. You will begin to see more initiative, higher production and quality because they will be working *más a gusto* (happier).

<u>Language variations</u>

Even the various dialects of the Spanish language can create conflict. To Mexicans, a *brazero* is a farm worker, whereas to an Argentine it's a barbecue or brassier. I recently learned that a *macho* is a man's man to a Mexican, a fair-skinned blonde man to a Costa Rican and a mule to a Nicaraguan!

Motivator: Concentrate on similarities, mutual goals and common objectives. Celebrate different cultures. A division of Greenlee-Textron has flags hanging from the rafters on the shop floor: one for every country the employees represent. Everyone is proud that "they all get along."

Offer programs that appeal to Hispanics' values

Realize that many Hispanic employees will miss a day or more of work due to family obligations in the U.S. or in their homelands. Female employees may miss work for childcare reasons. Help Hispanic employees become familiar with family leave laws, so they know their jobs will still be there when they return. Cross-train other employees to cover unexpected absences.

Now that you know that family is very important to Hispanics, consider offering childcare accommodations either at or near your site. This way, Mama or Papa can visit the children during the workday. What if your company can't afford the investment? As an alternative, provide an allowance so that a family member can take care of the children at or near the family's home.

Transportation is another big issue. Many Hispanics in manufacturing or service industries do not own a car. In a large city like Los Angeles, finding alternate transportation may not be a problem, but it could be in semi-rural and rural areas. Provide incentives for carpooling. Many states offer employer incentives for carpooling and other pollution-reducing modes of transportation like buses and bicycles. I used to work at Blue Cross of California where they offered a carpooling incentive of $25 per month.

Solicit the help of workplace "elders"

Sometimes you will have in your organization "unofficial leaders" who are either tenured employees or the most assimilated Hispanics. Utilize these individuals to distribute information or to assist you in reaching the masses. Many times the other workers will defer to the eldest Hispanic. This can be both good and bad for you. It's bad if their point-of-view, sense of urgency or agenda is different than yours, so you need to build relationships with these individuals.

Hire relatives of your Hispanic employees

Hiring relatives in the workplace is a great motivator. It promotes that feeling of family, especially if they come from a family of hard workers. You'll actually get peer pressure working on your side. It has been my experience that allowing Hispanic families to work at the same place creates good peer pressure, because honor is very big in the Hispanic culture. Members from the same family will not want to disgrace the family name. Cisco Brothers Furniture, for example, has nine sisters and their families at the company and it works very well.

On the other hand, I've also seen situations where families control the workplace and sabotage management's goals. To avoid this, you may want to only allow relatives to work for the same company as long as they work in different departments.

Offer Vocational English as a Second Language

Consider offering Vocational English as Second Language (VESL) classes or a trade apprenticeship or experiential skills program. You can also create career tracks, buddy systems and mentorship programs.

"Mentoring" is a big word in the Latino community. Use it often and back it up with formalized programs. The key to making it work with Latinos is to clarify that mentoring is a two-way street and that both the mentor and the Mentoree have equal responsibilities. This will create a participatory frame of mind, taking your organization from entitlement to enlightenment.

In 1962, Dr, Abraham H. Maslow, the psychologist well known for his work on motivation and personality, created the term "enlightened management," to describe the type of workplace that would be most conducive to the workers' reaching a point of self-actualization. It is this potential that you can tap into, while raising the trust level among Hispanic workers and management, stressing the need for honest recognition and the importance of continuous improvement.

Establish a baseline for performance to avoid the *Barbero* Syndrome

Peer pressure can work negatively in some places. It may be frowned upon to get too close to management or the *Americanos, gringos* or *Gavachos*. Some of the attitudes you might face include:

- "They are not to be trusted because they are management (or are different)."
- "They don't speak our language."
- "They don't understand our ways."
- "If you are not with us, you are against us."
- "Why should we work harder and give them more, when they aren't paying us any more?"
- "I could be making the same at the fast-food restaurant flipping burgers in an air-conditioned building. Why should I give them more?"

Anyone that crosses the line and starts to work harder or befriends management, or becomes part of management, will be chastised as a *barbero* (flatterer, kiss-up, brown-noser, etc.).

Combat this syndrome by involving everyone in establishing excellent levels of performance standards that can be objectively measured. Collecting baseline measures is usually a lot of hard work, particularly if there were no measurements previously. However, this is critical to your success and the success of your Hispanic employees.

Allow for sharing of leadership. Encourage new ideas. Have regular meetings in which you share information that affects the bottom line. Praise the group for a job well done. Don't single anyone out, as they might be chastised later as a *barbero*.

"Catch them doing something right"

Offer Hispanic employees positive feedback, encouragement, reinforcement and certificates of completion. Positive reinforcement on the job will go a long way towards boosting the self-esteem of your employees. A certificate is coveted, because it signifies education. Make certifying a "big deal" in your organization. Cal Western Paints pays employees that take a yearly 40-hour training program a higher salary.

Examples of empowerment at work

Example One

Twenty employees of a printing and graphics company were divided up into three task teams. One group logged the number of times and the cost associated with remaking printing plates due to internal errors, scheduling problems and client requests. The cost to the company was $6000 per month! Once this figure was discovered, the group took the initiative and conducted a Pareto cause and effect analysis. (According to the Pareto principle, 80 percent of your problems are caused by 20 percent of your processes, quality control systems, etc.) Although these employees were not familiar with the Pareto concept at first, when this tracking technique was explained using home-life examples they were able to catch on quickly.

When the task group reported their findings to everyone, a woman was unsure if she understood correctly. "You mean that these are costs that can't be passed on to the client and directly affect the company's bottom line?" she asked. "If so, what can we all do to prevent this loss?" As you can see, employees will pleasantly surprise you if you give them a chance and the right tools to understand.

Example Two

I conducted an 80-hour curriculum for Firecraft Technologies on effective communications, teambuilding, empowerment, problem-solving and lean manufacturing curriculum. The 22-team leaders were mostly Hispanic men who were first generation Hispanics with limited English-language skills.

As we were completing week six of the training, the team leaders still did not believe that management wanted to empower them. They were in disbelief and denial. They were afraid to move forward and take the initiate for fear of retribution or termination.

Management wanted more decisions being made at the lowest level in the organization. This would allow the existing mid-level supervisors to concentrate on more strategic goals and objectives for the company. For whatever reason, the goal to empower the team leaders was not clearly communicated, so I needed a "champion" with credibility to deliver the message. My champion was a third generation non-Spanish-speaking Hispanic, the plant's general manager. He arrived armed with transparencies of the company's quarterly profit & loss statement. These unsophisticated, hard working Hispanic team leaders were able to understand the financial statements and immediately started looking for ways to identify ways to make a difference; in this case, it was waste management. By the end of the class they identified nearly a dozen potential causes of waste and began implementing ways to eliminate this waste.

Empowerment 101

Test your company's readiness to empower Hispanic workers by answering these questions:

- Do we understand the ethnic and cultural differences between mainstream Americans and Hispanics?
- Do we recognize that there are different levels of assimilation among Hispanics? (recent immigrant vs. U.S.-born first generation vs. second generation)
- Do we participate in community outreach programs?
- Do we have strategic partners within the Hispanic community?
- Do we nurture long-term relationships?
- Do we understand the different views of time, body language, personal space and eye contact?
- Do we understand the concepts of elders, formality and respect?

Become familiar with common Spanish greetings, influential Hispanics and Latino civil rights organizations

Greetings

Buenos días	Good morning
Buenas tardes	Good afternoon
Buenas noches	Good night

Que le vaya bien   May you have good
fortune (used when departing)
Que Dios lo bendiga   May God bless you
– (reserved for more formal occasions)

Influential and Historical Hispanics

Cesar Chavez | Migrant farm worker, organizer and civil rights activist. He formed the National Farm Workers Association in 1965.

Rodolfo "Corky" Gonzalez | Boxer, poet and organizer of the first Chicano Youth Liberation conference

Jose Angel Gutierrez | Organizer of La Raza Unida political party

Dr. Juan Andrade, Jr. | Executive director of the U.S. Hispanic Leadership Institute

Elfero Baca | Famous lawman in New Mexico

Dr. Hector Garcia | Recipient of the Medal of Freedom from President Reagan in 1984

Antonia Pantoja | Educator and social worker who was

	instrumental in the birth of the National Puerto Rican Forum
Gloria Molina	Supervisor of the County of Los Angeles
Gloria Estefan	Singer and recording artist
Vickie Carr	Singer, recording artist and executive director of the Vickie Carr Foundation
Cruz Bustamente	Lieutenant governor of the State of California
Aida Alvarez	Administrator of the Small Business Administration (member of the President's cabinet)

Besides knowing some Hispanic role models and leaders, it's important that you know Latino organizations.

You may want to tap into these organizations locally for advice, potential employees, or to contribute to their scholarship funds. This is motivating to Hispanic employees when they know that your organization is supporting "the cause". The cause is the advancement of the Latino way of life, its culture and heritage, including our struggles to succeed in the U.S.

The organizations below promote Hispanics in a positive light, protect their civil rights are advocates and promote education.

American GI Forum
ASPIRA (translated it means Aspire)
Cuban-American National Council
League of United Latin American Citizens (LULAC)
Liga Puertorriqueña e Hispana
Mexican American Legal Defense and Educational Fund (MALDEF)
National Council of La Raza (NCLR)
Puerto Rican Legal Defense and Education Fund (PRLDEF)

Why is it important to know these things? The more you know, the more you will be able to understand and solidify your Hispanic relationships.

Understand how Latinos view themselves

In order to better understand the Latino community, I have listed below some feelings that we have about ourselves. Some reflect our insecurity; others reflect the pride we have in our family and heritage. My intent was to let you take a peek inside the psyche, or mind of the Latino to understand what might be going on inside your employee's head.

Armed with this information, you can adjust your management style accordingly to drive home your message in a culturally appropriate manner;

leverage your talent, increasing communication, cooperation, collaboration and trust.

- "I'm proud to be Latino."
- "I am 'the man of the family'."
- "I'm different."
- "I look different."
- "I talk different."
- "Being poor is virtuous."
- "Whatever God wills."
- "It is virtuous to suffer."
- "My parents are not educated."
- "I may not be educated, but I am an honest, hard working man."
- "Sweat is a measure of good honest work."
- "Ambition is not a virtue; it is greed."
- "It's not good manners to boast."
- "I'm a minority. This means second class."
- "I'm a minority. This means automatic discrimination."
- "I am grateful for my job."
- "It's an honor to have work."
- "I am obligated to you, my boss, for giving me a job."
- "I am afraid of you, my boss, because you hold my fate."
- "I will not give suggestions unless I am asked, for fear of retribution (*me corren*)."
- "I don't want to rock the boat or I'll be fired."
- "Family is everything."
- "Our children are our future."

Participate in community outreach programs

Once you know the Hispanic organizations in your community, you may want to sit on a Board of Directors. You may wish to create or contribute to scholarships and mentoring programs. Hispanic employees will respect you and your organization when they know you're giving back to their community. Hispanic employees themselves can also get involved with these organizations and serve as a cross-cultural bridge for your organization. Or they may wish to participate in mainstream organizations such as, the March of Dimes, Diabetes Foundation, Red Cross or the United Way. Many companies use fundraisers as a way to build company morale.

Your company could also implement a community outreach program to address any one of the following: personal growth and self-esteem, goal setting, leadership, collaboration, health access, cross-cultural communications, education or technology.

Chapter 4

Recruiting and Interviewing Hispanic Job Candidates

According to the magazine *Fast Company*, people are a critical asset in any organization, so much so that many companies now list employees as an "intellectual asset" on their financial statements.

The quality, skill and talents of your employees will determine whether your organization is able to meet its business objectives. It is the interviewer's job to hire the most qualified person for the job. When a person is hired, your company invests time, money and other resources to train and develop the new associate. Experts say that it costs a typical company more than $5000 to hire one individual. In order to make the most of your investment, managers need to make the best selection decision possible.

In order to motivate Hispanic employees, you need to hire motivated Hispanic employees. This chapter deals with the ideal profile you want to recruit. The more specific the traits and attributes for the specific job, the better quality individual you will recruit. Even if it's a simple job, you want to make sure you have a good match from the beginning. If the ideal candidate profile is not available in your area's labor pool, then this is how you want to develop the Hispanic employees in your organization.

The way managers conduct interviews plays an important role in hiring the best person for the job. See if your interviewing skills need polishing by answering these questions:

TRUE or FALSE

1. _____   Current job descriptions and specifications are the basics for the selection process.

2. _____   The interviewer should keep an open mind regarding the type of person needed for the job.

3. _____   It is a good idea to spend 5-10 minutes establishing rapport with the candidate.

4. _____   The interviewer should be listening about 80 percent of the time.

5. _____   You can encourage candidates to elaborate their answers by keeping silent or through noncommittal remarks.

6. _____   You can probe for detailed information by asking the pointed questions.

7. _____   When deciding on a candidate,

compare the candidates to each other, not just to the job specifications.

8. _____ You should only be concerned with the Hispanic applicant's technical qualifications and not motivation or attitude.

9. _____ Interviewers are responsible for telling candidates about the job and the company.

10._____ How you document the selection process is important.

Answers:
1. F-Task & activities are the basics
2. F-You need to know precisely
3. T
4. T
5. T
6. T-It's good to ask pointed, based on previous experience, but not leading questions
7. T
8. F
9. T
10.T

Planning

Finding the right candidate for the job requires planning. You must first determine the job requirements based on tasks and activities for the job, recruit candidates, and then screen the candidates. If written job requirements are not available at your company, you can often glean them from position descriptions. Another method to determine job requirements is to shadow your best employee in that position and create a profile of tasks and activities. You may also want to ask other similar businesses, your trade association, or labor unions.

A job description contains the following information in detail:

- Major functions
- Major responsibilities
- Priority of each responsibility

Here is an example of a job description for a receptionist:

Position title: Receptionist

Salary range: $_____

Major functions:

Contributes or directly supports the
  Entire company.

Answers and routes telephone calls courteously and efficiently.
Greets clients and visitors. Distributes and prepares mail. Prepares reports.

Job responsibilities	Duties Time percentage
Answers and routes Calls	Answers calls by the third ring. 60% Greeting should include: - "Good morning/afternoon" - Company name - "How may I help you?" Route all incoming calls. If transfer is unsuccessful, ask the caller if they want voicemail; otherwise take accurate message and route appropriately. Finds and trains quality replacement when temporarily away from position.
Greets clients courteously and promptly	Greets clients 20% Acknowledges clients even if busy with something else. Offers clients refreshment or restrooms.

Must be knowledgeable of personnel,
their   positions, departments and extensions.

Distributes mail and
delivery and distributes
to cubbies adjacent
to main switchboard.

Accepts mail 15%
Weighs and applies
postage to outbound
mail.

Accepts inbound faxes and distributes to cubbies adjacent to main switchboard.

Maintains centralized information,
policies and procedures manuals, shipping log, pages over intercom, etc.

Maintains front desk supplies as needed.

Completes Special projects as needed

Prepares reports as needed.   5%

Are you surprised at the depth of this job description? You shouldn't be.

All positions should have specific and measurable job requirements. This is especially critical in giving the Hispanic employee direction and instruction in quality customer service standards. By putting the job description in writing, both you and the Hispanic employee know what is expected.

When determining job descriptions, it is also important to make sure they are in line with the law. Can the qualifications be applied in the same way to everyone being interviewed and evaluated? Is the position equally open to minorities, women and the disabled? Are the job qualifications directly tied to the specifics of the job? Refer to the Appendix A to learn more about the Equal Employment Opportunity (EEO) and Americans with Disabilities Act 1990 (ADA) requirements.

Use the worksheet below to determine specific job requirements for any position in your organization.

Job requirement worksheet

Position to be filled:
   a) Name or unit or department:
   b) Location:
   c) Reporting relationship:

Job tasks:

Responsibilities:

Interaction: (Whom does the person interact with?)

Accountability (describe)
   a) Would they generate revenue?
   b) Would they provide or facilitate information?
   c) Do they provide customer relations?
   d) Do they process expenses?
   e) Do they manufacture or work at a process? (assembly, food service, etc.)

Job environment
   a) Conditions surrounding work area
   b) What hours are worked?
   c) Environment conditions (smoking, noise, heat, cold)
   d) Are there special requirements? (technical, trade, heavy lifting)
   e) Special schedule or work hours (travel, night work, long hours, other)

Competency requirements
   a) What skills are needed? (adequate, competent, exceptional)
   b) What attributes must they possess? (technical, trade, customer focus)
   c) What interpersonal skills must they possess? (outgoing, able to work alone)
   d) What knowledge is required?

e) How are the skills acquired (technical school, special courses, on-the-job training)

Managers should also determine qualification factors for each position. These include work experience, education and core competencies that are necessary to fill a position.

Work experience

Here, you are looking for experience in a trade or a professional background that relates directly or indirectly to the position. As an example, of you are hiring for a customer service position, you may consider an applicant with a retail sales background. Many of the same basic skills would transfer to your customer service position. When reviewing the job experience of an applicant, look for the following:

- What were the specific duties performed in previous jobs (supervised staff, served customers, managed workflow, completed spreadsheets, assembled fiber-optic connectors)
- What was the scope of the responsibilities? (technical, counter work, etc.)
- Are there any indicators of stable employment? (Have they worked for each company for a least one-year?) Early on in their job experience, Hispanic employees may hold many jobs on their way up the work experience ladder. Sometimes this is due to low wages, so they may have a

number of employers. I remember my Dad working three jobs when I was young. He did this in order to keep my mother home and to provide for the family.

Education

There are positions that may require degree or special courses (i.e. sheet metal operator, personal computers, accounting, and bookkeeping). Remember, 43 percent of U.S. Hispanics do not have a high school degree, so you must rely on past job experience and existing core competencies, OR you may be willing to train. If this is the case, the more formalized the training and orientation process the better for your organization in the long run. Here are some questions to ask yourself:

- What education is required?
- What education, specialized course work or work experience is mentioned in their resume?
- What work-related activities have been performed outside of work or school? (I know a gentleman who works at a fast-food restaurant because of his education level, yet he holds a leadership position at his local church. In my opinion, he could become and succeed in a work environment as lead person, foreman or supervisor.)

Hispanics applying for entry-level positions may not have resumes. In this case, rely on the application form and the personal interview. This can be challenging if the candidate does not speak English. You may want to hire a bilingual person for your main office or human resources department to assist you in translating. Another option would be to have a Spanish-speaking supervisor from the floor assist you in the interview process. Be creative in making the interview process easier, but stay within legal and privacy guidelines. Make sure your front office staff treats potential candidates with respect and in a friendly courteous manner.

Core Competencies

Positions often require special skills such as technical, interpersonal or supervisory skills. Refer to your job description to determine what specifics are required.

- What pertinent technical skills are mentioned in the resume or application?
- What business knowledge is required to perform the job?

Interview for Experiential Qualities

Experiential characteristics are those observable qualities that will directly enhance job performance. Suppose, for example, that you have a job with tasks that might change periodically as a result of new equipment, seasonality, customer demands or procedures. You should consider an applicant who demonstrates an ability to be flexible and adept to the changing work environment.

Work experience, education and competencies can come together in a Qualification Analysis. A qualification analysis is used to match the Hispanic employee's qualifications to the specific needs and requirements of the position. The column on the left lists the required job requirements a work experience or characteristics that you may be looking for in a candidate. In this case, lead person/punch press operator combination. The column on the right might be a note the interviewer writes to themselves about the potential candidate's qualifications.

Sample Qualification Analysis

Job requirements
Candidate's qualifications

Take a look at required work experience:

Two years supervisory assistance in
One year as assistant supervisor in
related field a sheet metal company

Experience in training staff. Two years training staff on job procedures & equipment and safety
Desired work experience:

One year work leader experience in
One year as assistant supervisor in
sheet metal setting.
Experience in self-directed teams,
Has worked in teams.
Last employer allowed teams to implement improvement projects.

What is the required education:

> High school preferred, but will also
> accept technical school or 3-5 years
> work experience. Remember many Latinos
> will not have a high school degree, but may
> have the necessary work experience.

> You notes might say:
> No HS degree, but has TQM, TPM
> or teambuilding course-work
> related experience
> completed at last job. Certified
> Forklift driver.

Desired work experience:

> CNC and Punch press
> Also Cincinnati grinder.

> Your notes might say:
> Operations and supervisory training
> Completed production paperwork
> Skills in last job, responsible for scheduling
> Employees and vacations.
> Can operate CNC and Punch press

Required core competencies:

> Training skills
> People skills
> Able to work in a team environment
> Operations
> Manufacturing die set-up testing
> Coordinate work to staff.

Your notes might say:
States has cross- trained staff in last job.
Has PC experience
held position as assistant supervisor/lead
Scheduling person.

Labor law

Has attended several supervisory and TQM
courses and seminars.

Experiential characteristics:

Communicates well
Bilingual. Spoke clearly and was
Organized.
Easily understood by interviewer.
Resourceful figured out how to produce
multiple pieces utilizing one die at last job.
Thinks on their feet
Demonstrated initiative
Friendly responses to specific work-related,
detail-oriented questions. Gave detailed
answers.
Good listener
Didn't finish my sentences. Asked me
for clarification several times.
Patient
Did not seem flustered that interview
started 15 minutes late.

Recruiting

Once you have determined the job requirements,
you are ready to recruit candidates for the

position. Potential candidates can come from a variety of sources:

Internal candidates

This is almost always one of the best recruiting methods, as it boosts the morale of your current employees. Associates see positions filled through transfers or promotions. This sends a message that management is committed to helping its employees in furthering their careers and rewards performance.

Application and resume files

Your city's employment office and your company's human resources manager receive applications and resumes on a daily basis. Applicants on file may have been tested for basic skills or prescreened by an employment recruiter or hiring manager.

Community outreach

Churches, Latino organizations and Hispanic leaders in the community are good sources for potential candidates. Get involved with your local Hispanic Chamber of Commerce or LULAC chapter by attending meetings, building relationships with members or sponsoring events. Take a look at other businesses (banks, investment companies, hospitals, etc.) that are already sponsoring events in the Hispanic community, and either attend or piggy-back to reduce your recruitment costs...

Recruit at your local community colleges and high schools. Don't forget the local trade techs, unions and trade associations.

Make connections with local mainstream organizations that sponsor scholarships targeted at Latino students.

Advertising

Advertising is one of the most commonly used recruiting methods, as it usually brings in the highest number of applicants. However, I would recommend using this method only as a last resort. Unfortunately, the majority of applicants that respond to an ad tend not to be adequately qualified. To minimize the number of non-qualified respondents, tailor your ad to fit the open position. Consider your audience. Choose a newspaper or trade journal that will provide the best exposure to your audience of potential candidates. You may also wish to take out a Spanish ad in the local Spanish-language paper or Hispanic Chamber of Commerce newsletter. (I suggest you submit the ad in English and let the newspaper translate in into Spanish, there's usually no charge to translate the ad if you're placing it in their publication.)

Aside from deciding which publication to use, you should also consider when to advertise and where to position the ad in the paper. Sunday is usually the best day to advertise in local papers. Tuesday is the preferred day for advertising in the *Wall Street Journal*. Saturday is good day for Latino newspapers because the family is planning the evenings weekly outing. Ads can be placed in the classified section, but take care when choosing a heading. Maybe the ad will get more exposure if it appears under "insurance" rather than "healthcare." Again, remember to think about the target audience, or Machinist rather than bilingual supervisor.

The ad itself, or the message, is just as important as the placement. Pay attention to the wording and overall appearance of the employment ad. Since ads are expensive, poorly written ones are a waste of your company's money. Think about the image your company wants to portray in print. What will attract people to answer the ad? What will accurately reflect job duties and qualifications? Make every word count!

Be careful that the language of the ad is scrupulously legal. Avoid mention of age or gender limitations. Make sure that the requirements you state are essential to the job. Watch that language does not commit the company. (For example, calling the job "permanent" and later having to terminate the position or employee. Use the terms "part-time" and "full time" instead.) Work with your human resources department to develop all employment ads. I recommend the book, *The Hiring, Firing and Everything Forms Book* by James Jenks.

Recruitment/ Temporary firms

Recruitment firms can also be referred to as personnel services, personnel agencies, employment agencies, recruiters or headhunters. There are literally thousands of these companies in the United States, attesting to the amount of business there is for them. A good agency can find quality candidates that are not actively seeking new employment. These are the people who are not reading classified ads.

Temporary agencies are a good source for getting to know your potential employees. Many companies hire on a temp to full time basis to make sure the new people fit into the corporate culture, and that they can perform adequately. Don't use the phrase: temp to perm, as it could be misconstrued as a warranty or guarantee of employment.

Direct sourcing and personnel recommendations

Direct sourcing (also known as "cold calling") is another effective method of recruiting people that are not actively looking for another job. Although effective, this method takes time, skill and creative networking.

Another method of direct sourcing is through personal observation. This happens when you either observe an employee that fits your ideal candidate profile, or when you receive exceptional service somewhere. Don't be afraid to ask the person if he or she is happy working there. Ask them if they might be interested in exploring other employment options.

Personnel recommendations (recommendations from existing employees) are very common among Hispanic candidates. Hispanics are very well networked. Doesn't it seem sometimes that some Hispanic employees have hundreds of cousins? A word of caution: Know the person who made the recommendation and ask some questions about the referral first. Then treat the referral as any other candidate: conduct a well-planned interview and check all references. Keep in mind that just because a good employee refers a candidate doesn't guarantee the candidate will provide the same caliber performance.

You might want to create an employee referral program that provides incentives for employees to refer candidates that will fit the job requirements and the company culture. This is why it's so important for your organization to develop sound job activity and task profiles. Make sure the policies of your employee referral program are in writing. I recommend giving the referring employee the agreed payment or other incentive only once the new hire has been with the company for 60-90 days.

Other sources

Sources of job candidates can also include open houses, career fairs, campus recruiting, professional associations, high school, trade school or college placement offices, senior centers and disabled congregate homes. (I've experienced some of the best service from Downs Syndrome employees).

Screening Hispanic candidates

<u>Telephone screening</u>

When a recruiting ad invites applicants to call for more information, the telephone call is the first step in interviewing and selection. Make sure that enough people in the office speak Spanish to make this method viable. Telephone screening gives you an opportunity to measure the Hispanic employee's telephone, comprehension and language skills. They are particularly useful when a position has attracted a large number of apparently qualified applicants. It is also preferable when a position has been advertised in out-of-town newspapers. Before incurring the expense of traveling to meet the applicant or having the candidate travel to the company's location, conduct a telephone interview to make sure the candidate meets your specific requirements.

After reviewing resumes and job applications, telephone screening can also be used as a "pre-interview." Except for walk-in candidates who may be seen briefly by an interviewer, all other candidates should be screened by phone to determine whether an in-depth interview is warranted. Culturally, Hispanics have no problem walking into a place of business without an appointment. It is honorable to search for work.

Sometimes an applicant's resume will not be particularly impressive. However, if he or she has been highly recommended, a telephone screening might be appropriate. Be prepared in some cases for Hispanic candidates that have no telephone available or are sharing a telephone with family: cousins, aunts, uncles, etc. If there is a language challenge, it's ok to ask if someone in the household speaks English and use them as a translator. You will need to be very patient and resourceful here. Simply ask your questions.

When interviewing by phone, use a prepared list of questions. Ask questions that will help you determine if the applicant has the qualifications that you are seeking. There's no need to keep saying: "ask Juan about"... The translator is simply a tool. If the applicant does not possess the necessary qualifications, the phone call can be ended quickly. However, if the answers are satisfactory, you should schedule a face-to-face interview.

In-person interviews

Skillful interviewing, whether by phone or in person, requires a systematic approach. The interview is a two-way process: you are interviewing the candidate and the candidate is interviewing you and your company. The objective of each interview is to gather enough pertinent information to make the best possible selection decision. This can be done by setting the climate, asking experiential questions and using follow-up techniques.

To put the candidates at ease, I suggest conducting the interview at a small round conference table. As Hispanics tend to sit more closely than the norm, sitting at a smaller table rather than across your desk will put the Hispanic candidate more at ease. Ask the candidates how much they know about the company and the position. Fill them in on both, if necessary, as a means of building rapport. Then move on to the meatier questions.

Encourage the applicants to do most of the talking. This is critical, since many managers tend to talk too much if they are nervous or inexperienced at conducting interviews. One way to elicit more than one-word answers from candidates is to use the FACT method of questioning.

FACT is a systematic and thorough approach to gathering work-related information about your Hispanic candidates. FACT stands for:

Feelings
Actions
Context
Thoughts

The idea is to learn about situations that the candidate recently encountered or experienced in a work environment, and probe for specifics about how he or she handled them. The candidate's responses will likely provide insight into his or her skill level, communication style and commitment level.

**Mark the correct letter in the box below.
Is it a:**

Feeling
Action
Context or
Thought

	List of common FACT gathering statements
	1. "Can you give me a picture of that?"
	2. "If I were there what would I see?"
	3. "Walk me through that (incident) (meeting) etc."
	4. "Can you give me an example of a time that you..."
	5. "Can you give me an example of such a (group) (meeting)?"
	6. "You said 'we'. What did you mean specifically? What part did you play?"
	7. "Can you tell me what you actually said to him/her?"
	8. "Can you tell me what you mean by...?"

	9. "That was a good overview. Now let's go back and get the details..."
	10. "How were you feeling then...?"
	11. "Tell me about a time when you..."
	12. "Take a minute to reflect. Then, give me a quick overview of the situation..."
	13. "What were the key events, the critical points along the way?"
	14. "How did it start?"
	15. "Tell me about ..."X". What led up to it?"
	"What were some of the specific things you talked about?"

Answers:

1.C	5.F	9. C	13.F
2.C	6.A	10.F	14.A
3.C	7.C	11.C	15.F
4.F	8.C	12.T	16.T

Here's the reasoning behind these questions:

Question 1: "Could you give me an overview of your current roles and responsibilities?"

(This question is designed to measure the scope of responsibility the candidate had at a previous job, which will provide the basis for the interview discussion.)

Question 2: "Now, let's focus on a key event that has recently happened to you at work...something you were involved with that went very well." OR "something that went poorly or not as well as you expected."

(You want to measure the level of accountability vs. blaming.)

Question 3: "Walk me through the situation....Tell me about your role in the situation."

(Having the candidate retell the situation or event step by step is called "cueing" them. By "reliving" it, the interviewer can often observe what might have been the candidate's reaction at the precise moment of the event, including stress in the voice, facial expressions, different breathing patterns, etc.)

Each time you get to a point you want to explore further, ask a probing question that requires the candidate to elaborate. Probing questions include:

- "You said...Let's go back to that, what was it like?"
- "What do you suppose prompted that reaction or situation?"
- "How did that make you feel at the time?"
- "How did you handle that particular situation or issue?"
- "Who else was involved?"
- "What kind of training had you received before then?"
- "Why did you make that decision?"

These questions probe the person's response, past behavior, actions, thoughts and feelings. You will find that the detailed information gathered will be useful to assess the person's competencies in a specific work situation or in fitting into your corporate or organizational culture. Also be sure to ask about the results or outcome of the situation you were discussing. This will provide insight as to the Hispanic candidate's ability to follow-through, his or her skill level, initiative and ability to meet deadlines.

Here's an example of how you might use the F.A.C.T. approach:

You Say: "Could you provide me an overview of your current roles and responsibilities?" (This question is designed to measure, in detail, the exact scope of responsibility the candidate had at a previous job, which will provide the basis for the interview discussion)

You Say: "Now, let's focus on a key event that has recently happened to you at work... Something you were involved with that went very well ... when you were satisfied with the results or outcome...? OR you might want to say, "Now, let's focus on a key event that has recently happened to you at work... Something you were involved with that went poorly or less than you expected?

WALK the person through the situation. This is called "cueing" so they actually take themselves back through time, reliving the particular situation. This type of technique is especially effective and currently used with seniors or Alzheimer's patients to stimulate very vivid memories of the past. When you cue someone using this method, you get to observe what might have been their reaction at that precise moment of time or series of events, including: stress in the voice, breathing patterns, feelings, eye dilation, etc. It's uncanny!

When interviewing a candidate, it is also useful to measure his or her core competencies. Core competencies are behaviors, habits and skills that are essential to perform the job well. The following tables will provide you with a way to measure and rate the Hispanic candidate's core competencies in the following areas:

- Business and knowledge
- Production Standards
- Self-development
- Customer focus
- Teamwork
- Achievement
- Implementing
- Planning

Business and Knowledge

Demonstrates a broad understanding of the organizational structure, including how management operates and makes decisions.

Identifies issues either within or outside the team that impede accomplishment of desired results.

Actively seeks and utilizes organizational resources and information.

Develops solutions aimed at breaking down barriers to meet individual and/or team objectives.

Production Standards

Measures the candidates understanding of their role as an employee.

Helps the employee understand that they will be utilized as a resource to make a profit for the company. Some Hispanic employees resent this, but this is the goal of business in a capitalistic society. Is it not?

Identifies the pace that the job will require, and any reporting to keep track of performance numbers.

Measures the candidate's ability to utilize different tools to complete the necessary work?

Also measure their ability to ask for the right tools. The more assimilated Hispanic employees will understand the value of asking for the right tools. The least assimilated Hispanic employees will be reticent about asking.

Self-development

The employee recognizes the need to adopt new behavior and approaches to improve oneself.

Is open to constructive criticism and suggestions to improve their job performance.

Asks for feedback on behavior and performance.

Analyzes own performance as well as feedback from others and takes measures to improve it.

Creates a plan for self-development, including specific improvement measures over time.

Customer Focus

Follows through on customer inquiries, requests and complaints.

Gives specific directions, full explanations and communicates possible courses of action to the customer.

Acknowledges the customer quickly and politely.

Spends the necessary time with customers to solve their problems and better serve their needs.

Demonstrates strong customer service traits.

Takes personal responsibility for promptly and effectively correcting customer problems, issues and concerns.

Actively works to identify changes or process improvements to better serve all customers.

Understands that he or she is a "Front-line Revenue Generator" and "markets" accordingly.

Teamwork

Actively participates in and promotes effective teamwork by readily accepting team assignments, participating in team goal-setting and decision-making.

Keeps other team members informed.

Expresses positive expectations of others in terms of their abilities, expected contributions, etc.

Actively sets an example by contributing maximum personal efforts and helping other team members to achieve group goals.

Creates a positive environment by promoting a sense of enjoyment and pride in belonging to the team.

Transfer this number to the Interview Rating Form to see the candidate's highest- and lowest-scoring areas.

Achievement

Strives to meet goals and deadlines. Follows through on commitments.

Questions the status quo in order to identify ways to improve methods, processes and approaches.

Establishes stretch goals for self that imply an improvement in performance over time (i.e. "when I took over efficiency was 20%, now it's 80 %")

Identifies and initiates new ideas and work methods.

Implementing

Understands and fully supports the plan through own words and actions.

Ensures others know how they fit into the plan and what they must do to achieve the organization's long-term goals.

Leads others and generates buy-in through regular meetings and other interactions.

Actively demonstrates full support for change by recognizing and rewarding others who participate in the change process.

Gains access to resources and information to benefit the team/division/unit/organization.

Knows how to use equipment safely, effectively and productively.

Planning

Sets specific, detailed priorities to focus efforts of team members or associates.

Designates work or project assignments in order to maximize current and future resources.

Make decisions on the basis of cost-benefit analysis.

Examines impact of current decisions on the future.

Is accountable for their own decisions.

Initiates plans to position the organization to effectively capitalize on challenges, even in the face of risk or resistance.

These profiles are designed to help you hire the right individuals and will help you in developing their individual growth even if you are looking strictly for laborers.

Summary Points:

Help the Hispanic candidate re-live (cue them) key events in the past or at their former jobs including:

- their actions
- thoughts
- patterns
- behaviors... (experiential events)

Paraphrase their responses for clarification... DO NOT Lead!

Get the F.A.C.T.S. Remember a large percentage of the Hispanic community is Visual, so ask visually appropriate questions, such as "What would I see", "Paint me a picture, etc." *Como viste la situacion?* "How did you see the situation?"

You ultimately will decide whom you hire. As you assess the level of competency then you will have a very good indicator of the amount of development time and money you will have to invest on each candidate.

Even if you are simply filling a fast-food position, these core activities provide you with the parameters a person must be capable of performing in order to be successful in their position. Below are some examples of core competencies you might be looking for in a Hispanic candidate. Each level provides decided experiential descriptions or success "indicators":

Examples might be:

Business knowledge- How much do they know about making a profit for the organization. If a non-profit, do they understand the purpose and the different types of non-profit organizations there advantages and disadvantages: 501(c) 3, 403 (b), 408(b), etc.)

Self-development- Have they made a commitment to continuous personal improvement?

Customer Focus -How does the employee treat internal and external customers?

Teamwork – Have they experienced group dynamics, such as consensus, or do they think it is a team because people are grouped together

Achievement- Does the candidate have that will, or *ganas*, to succeed?

Do they identifies and initiates new products and work methods, using new technologies, in order to improve performance.

Implementing- Do they know how to support a plan working through the proper channels in a constructive and effective manner?

Planning – Do they know how to set specific, detailed priorities to focus efforts of team members or associates?
Designate work or project assignments in order to maximize current and future resources.
Leadership- Can they direct, support and motivate others by facilitating others efforts directly and constructively?
Problem-solving - Considers options and alternatives about how to respond to immediate problem situations. Takes action and initiative in the diagnosis and solving of own problems. Offers specific recommendations based on perceived pros and cons of each alternative.

Conducting the Interview

Provide Information and Conclude

This stage moves quickly. The purpose of providing information to the applicant is to ask questions about the job and for you to realistically sell the company and the job.

Specifically, in this stage, you will specifically:

1. Answer the candidate's questions about the job and the company.
2. Summarize the primary responsibilities and qualifications for the position.
3. Discuss opportunities and benefit provided by the company.
4. (If appropriate discuss salary).
5. Conclude the interview.

Concluding leaves the applicant with a final and favorable impression of your company.

Specifically, in this stage you will:

1. Describe the next step in the interview process, which is to continue interviewing or evaluating various other candidates.
2. Thank the applicant for their time.

Five points for interviewing a Super-Star Employee:

Self-Reliance

Success   Persistence

Potential   Knowledge

- Identify the knowledge and the skills required doing a job well, so the Hispanic employee can become self-reliant and productive.
- Hire for potential growth
- Create interview questions that assess quality skills.
- Use current job description and list of essential job functions (tasks and activities) as well as other information gathered.

Combined Categories of knowledge:

Prospecting, telephone skills, securing appointments, initial contacts, follow-up, understanding and tracking "their numbers", etc.

Creating Job Knowledge Questions:

- Knowledge currently & previously used
- Knowledge previously required
- Frequency/Duration prior to employment
- What are the Critical or Essential job descriptions?

Creating Job Knowledge Questions:

Ask about actual job experience or formal training. (experiential behaviors)

Ask about certification requirements or special licenses in previous job.

Think of questions that ask how the employee previously handled certain problems: people, boss, schedule, etc.

Ask questions that test for different levels of skill & commitment:

"What would you do if..."

"Tell me about...yourself or a time when..."

Evaluation

The evaluation process is the final step in the selection process. The three keys to ensure effectiveness here are to:

- Immediately evaluate the candidate after the interview.
- Avoid evaluation pitfalls, and
- Match the right person to the job.

Key #1   Immediate Evaluation

The sooner you document the interview information, the more accurate you will be in evaluating and remembering the candidate's qualifications. Studies indicate that even one interruption, such as a phone call, can reduce the ability to remember the information learned in the interview.

Re-read your interview notes. Record any additional job-related observations you recall.

Example:

The candidate was very articulate throughout the interview.

Compare your interview notes with the Qualification Analysis on page 120, with your colleague who was the observer. Note how the two match, then determine how the candidate meets the qualifications of the job.

Immediately record the information you've gained about the applicant in your "Interview Summary."

An interview summary is simply your record of your comments or impressions made during the interview that relate to the

Qualification Analysis:

List in factual terms what you heard and observed from the applicant, rather than your feelings or assumptions about the person.

For example: "lacks confidence" is an opinion, NOT a fact!

Refer to the Competency Requirements of the job and note your observations accordingly.

Assess and Select Candidates

Key #2   Avoid Evaluation Pitfalls

Assessment pitfalls are mistakes and interviewer can make that may distort the applicant's true qualifications for the job

Key #3:   Assessing the Candidate
Match the Right Person to the Job

Assess all the job candidates to determine the best match for the job. Compare the job requirements to each candidate's qualifications and rank each candidate based on the requirements.

A "Candidate Requirement Summary" can help you rank the candidates from 1-5 in terms of meeting job requirements. You can make your own headings which should include the likelihood of their success to certain criteria.

After ranking the candidates based on their qualifications, consider these questions:

Does the highest ranked person possess the "critical Competencies" qualifications to perform the job? If so, do you feel a match exists?

If a candidate does not have all of your "musts", you have a decision to make:

Continue sourcing candidates, or lower the minimum qualifications and provide on-the-job training.

Evaluation pitfalls are mistakes and interviewer can make that may distort the applicant's true qualifications for the job. Think about the following pitfalls.

The Halo Effect

It's normal to "root for the underdog" or want people to do well in an interview. Resist this temptation. Keep an objective mind.
Keep focused on the qualities (traits/attributes) that you are looking for.

First Impression

If the person is articulate, or dresses well, we may automatically assume that the rest of the "package" is fine. Take my word: I have made the mistake of hiring people that look good, smell good, etc., but when it came time to "dig in" with results, they were not able to perform.

Similarity to the interviewer

It's human to like people that are like us. Again, resist this temptation: get past your ego, avoid being flattered, and focus on the candidate's qualifications:

The person's skills, past success behaviors/indicators, talents and other "indicators" that match your job requirements.

Be Objective!

Match the person to the job by focusing on qualifications!

Making the Offer:

IN EVERY SELECTION PROCESS, the company selects the person just as the person selects the company. There must always be a match of "NEEDS" – organizational and personal.

Don't wait too long to make the offer. After interviewing and reference checking, the offer should be made within a few days (not weeks). Good Hispanic candidates will not want to be unemployed for very long, usually they may even have several companies pursuing them simultaneously.
Let the candidate have a few days (a week or two at the most) to review the offer. Do not rely on their follow-up. Solid business telephone follow-up skills are not normally part of the Hispanic community. There is also a barrier of embarrassment. "Me da pena llamar". I'm embarrassed to call... So you need to take the initiative.

Exceptions are those jobs that need to be filled immediately.

Confirm the offer with a phone call and in writing. Make sure that anything is put in writing to an associate is something the company can live with for the duration of the associate's employment. Contact your attorney or human Resources

Department for sample letters. (Or see James Jenks' book).

Clarify employment details with candidate. Starting salary, attire, etc. This information should be part of this information. Send materials to the candidate about the company and the job to begin and orientation process. (Drug testing, etc.)

Notify the people NOT SELECTED.

In closing, you want to create task & activity descriptions rather than "job descriptions."

Now that you have some understanding of the ethnic, cultural, motivational,
sensitivity and perception factors you are ready to create some foundational or fundamental procedures for creating "career paths" to groom future supervisors and managers!

Provide ongoing formal education, technical training including On-the-job-training (OJT), to raise the business literacy and skill level of Hispanic employees.

Be persistent. These changes may take some time, but once you have a few successes and they become part of your company's fabric and culture, then you will be on the "fast track" to Motivating Hispanic Employees.

Motivator:

Learn to speak Spanish. That is to say, it's a compliment to your Hispanic employees when you try to speak the language or pick up on some of the culture. The best example I've seen is a fully bilingual Chinese Human Resources manager at Prime Wheel in Los Angeles, CA. Be sensitive, and respectful. In an appropriate setting, such as a party, it may be ok for you to put on a serape or a sombrero, but only if invited to do so. (Use your better judgement, you know your employees best). It also goes a long way when you can be a real person. Kid around subtly. It may be considered a lack of decorum if you act too much like "one of the compadres".

Latinos like riddles, poems, quotes, or dichos (sayings). Use these often. Learn when they are appropriate to illustrate a position, or to punctuate a point, or sentiment.

For example, when you want to rally the troops and there are little funds in your budget, you lay out the plan and punctuate with a "call to action" by saying something like:

"Well, I know this is a challenge for us all given the small budget or lack of funds, but I know I can count on you to reduce costs, or increase productivity, or whatever, in order to accomplish our goals. As they say," 'de tripas, se hace chorizo.' Then watch your employee's faces light up! Now you've got them "fired up", in a good way!

This saying (dicho) translates into: "Sausage is made from scraps of meat". I know it loses its impact in English, but I think you'll agree that the concept is powerful!

By the way, many of you probably know other "dichos" or street vernacular. I don't recommend your using these obscenities in the workplace. You may think this is fine, but the level of respect and trust toward you from Hispanic employees will drop dramatically. Hispanics have a need to maintain formal lines of authority seeing you in the Jefe (Boss) position.

Sense of Humor

Hispanic employees will appreciate appropriate humor used at the appropriate times. Hispanic employees will talk about how you are "too serious" if you don't use humor. You have an opportunity to use humor as a motivator, making yourself more approachable, and hence, creating more dialogue. One short note and that is that the higher on the acculturation chart the Hispanic, the easier it will be for them to understand "dry' humor. Dry humor is not normally part of the Hispanic heritage. Enjoy and have fun. Keep a good sense of humor about you.

Ultimately it is your decision to hire the right person for the job. I understand that sometimes you may not have the luxury of being selective, but believe me; you will save yourself lots of time and aggravation by investing time up front.

Remember the 1 to 3 Rule says, that for every minute, hour, etc, we spend up front; we save 3 minutes, hours, etc. on the back end.

Secondly, in the Hispanic market you will have to contend with language and literacy issues. If you decide to hire regardless of competencies, then you must have an infrastructure or "success track in place that addresses developing the employee to the next level of excellence. Otherwise you are setting yourself and the Hispanic employee up for failure.

This system obviously works very well in profiling all new potential employees, not just Hispanic candidates.
However, the numbers speak for themselves. Forty-six percent of the 35 U.S. Latinos do not have a high school degree. This translates to about 15 million Latinos. America cannot afford to have these many under-educated employees as this population segment explodes.

Where will your company's next leaders come from, where will your next strategic partners come from? We will all reap great rewards as we invest in educating this hardworking population segment.

Please see page Appendix A for hiring practices as defined by the Americans with Disabilities Act. (ADA)

Chapter 5

Setting and Measuring Goals & Objectives

No baseline measure, essentially means no performance measurement system!

In an earlier chapter we talked about the importance of setting a baseline for performance.

We have worked hard to develop Hispanic employees up to this point in time, and performance measures equate to a roadmap for success. You got to have performance measures!

Remember that as a community we work very hard, but many don't know how to work "smart" or how to achieve effectively. There are lots of successes. Don't get me wrong, but many can be at a higher level of if more effective ways are shared.

A recent Spanish language BMW automotive ad featured a shiny red convertible sports car with the Spanish saying: "Querer is poder", which translated means "to achieve is to want". This image stirs the desire in anyone, but hits deep traditions and lifestyle issues for Hispanics. To a Hispanic, owning this type of car becomes a pinnacle status symbol of achievement. The ad is effective in making Hispanics "want" the car, but the caption still fuels the misconception within the community which would be more properly addressed as: "Hacer is Poder", which translates to do, or act is to achieve. Quite a play on semantics here, but I'm hoping you see, and understand the fine nuance in the Hispanic programming logic. BMW understands this faulty programming and then address the issue in their ad copy when translated says:

"...so if you want to drive your own BMW, we'd like to tell you how you can get one...

Your position as a leader in your organization then becomes how to show Hispanic employees what you want them to do and how to do it, and you have to use relational and emotional methods rather than a rational methods.

You need to know about the triangular thinking that is deeply rooted within this culture.

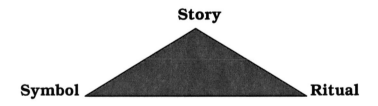

Source: Dr. Tom A. Steffan, Biola School of Intercultural Studies

The stories create movement. It's the "how to" in the above scenario. You cannot be abstract here or you will lose the Hispanic employee. Use stories and metaphors, not statistics.

The symbol becomes the car itself, which was featured in the previous ad, is the symbol of success. So it's the symbol for many individuals, you might say. Yes, it is, but for Latinos it's like looking way up trying to see the top of Mt. Everest. There are other symbols within the Hispanic community, which has already become part of the fabric. Family, statues or decals of saints on machinery, cars or front lawns are some of these symbols. In the workplace, the symbol might be status as a successful employee, or manager.

The rituals are the heritage or customs such as eating congregate or communal meals, talking loudly or all at once, dancing, Mariachi music, Baptisms, weddings, quinceñera celebrations (debutante), religious holidays, funerals, etc. These are key milestones and traditions in the Hispanic community. In the workplace, these would be congregate meals, problem solving together, and hierarchy of rank or tenure. (Respect and deference to the eldest employee)

A tradition acts like an anchor that gives organization and a sense of history and destiny. It tends to pacify some Hispanics that desire order, and crave predictability and stability.

As a manager, we need to assist the Hispanic employee pick up their anchor during work hours while being sensitive and allowing them to drop anchor again at the end of the workday, keeping their dignity in tact. You can create a win-win situation by modifying your systems or processes to reinforce this sense of order, predictability and stability. We can do this by appealing and teaching through the heart to get to the brain.

You have to appeal to this triangular thinking so that you can develop a deep relationship, transitioning to shared leadership assisting them in visualizing their potential so that the Hispanic employee can own their vision. Finally, you have to model the behavior that you want. You got to walk your talk!

If they respect you, they will follow you!

Remember: It's Relational NOT Rational

Hispanics are highly Visual

When you show Hispanic employees the how to, show it in written form, or through pictures. The Hispanic community is very visual, so if you want to get it done, show it in picture form. Then track it in picture form: graphs, charts, trend lines, etc.

This is so important that one of my earlier clients, The Los Angeles County Fairplex switched their on-site signage from words to pictures at their concession stands, and doubled their concession revenues from one year to the next!

Additionally, you need to ask people for what you want. Notice that I did not say "tell" people what you want. Hispanics don't like being told, but they like being "asked" in a polite way. You need to specify state what exactly it is that what you want done.

Remember when you where a kid and your parents told you not to play in the street. What would you do? – Play in the street that's right! Not because the seed had been planted, but because the instructions and boundaries had not been clearly defined, or specific enough. This is the same thing with Hispanic employees. You need to ask exactly what it is that you want, at what level of quality, and at what level of output. You provide the tools and skills necessary to do it, and then you measure, and measure, and measure.

It doesn't matter if you are service provider or a manufacturer. When you collect baseline information and you establish a starting point, then you can measure and compare subsequent changes, trends and improvements!

A trend is a measure that shows how something is doing over time by comparing and activity, output, or accomplishment. This is why it's critical to switch from job descriptions to activity descriptions. You can measure activity!

Trending can measure specific performance levels over a specified period of time: A week, a month, a quarter, a year, etc.

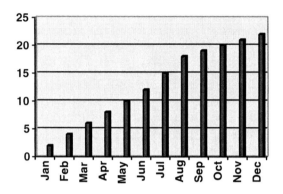

┌────────────────────────────┐
│   **2000 YTD Sales**   │
└────────────────────────────┘

The graph above illustrates a trend in sales for a Hispanic sales force for the year 2000. The trend shows steady upward growth, but exponentially the last few months experienced a lesser percentage gain than the earlier months. There are many factors that may affect this. Your job as a manager is to find out why?

There are many approaches which we can take, but basically, the point I wanted to make is that by having an initial baseline production in the above example, then we can measure the differential, or "performance gap" over time, and then against different windows of time. For example, how did we do this October as compared to last October or two years ago, October.

You set the priorities, but be willing to negotiate:

Different variables may ultimately affect the outcome, including shifts in the competition. I guess a good way to say it, would be that you cannot afford to be a stagnant organization, in order to compete effectively in today's business environment your business, and employees, must be dynamic and agile!

The priorities you set will be determined by a couple of factors. First are the organizational goals and objectives. When the enterprise creates these, the rest of the organization must align their efforts to roll up to feed into, or reinforce the enterprise goals.

These need to be measured and reported to Hispanic employees quarterly! When information is shared, trust and motivation rise.

Determine key result areas:

Assign a weighted percentage.
For example, let's say we have a new product at our plant. The competition is fierce, and we need to add more employees.

We've done our research and development now it's time to produce.

What's more important? How do we determine which of the three variables is most important?

The weighted percentage may look like this:

New Product	Rollout	60%
Competition	Research & Report	20%
Hire Employees	Begin Hiring	20%

We now have committed ourselves and our resources to follow a specific tack, where the majority of our time and the time of our resources will go towards getting the new product out.

This percentage commitment is great because the percentage can be translated to many variables including, our time, finances, and other resources.

Let's say that three months later, we find out your competition is working on a similar product:

We may then want to switch our course of action to:

New Product	Rollout	20%
Competition	Research & Report	60%
Hire Employees	Begin Hiring	20%

Each time there is change in direction you must advise Hispanic employees, so that everyone can allocate their time appropriately. Remember Hispanic tradition dictates order, predictability and stability. These are not congruent in today's fast-paced competitive world. Get Hispanic Employees used to continuous change, so everyone becomes adaptable and agile. Remember Hispanic sense of time does not tolerate quick or constant changes. This is going to cause lots of conflict and trepidation in your workplace, so you must communicate constantly, especially if you *anticipate* any change.

Think about how fast-paced today's marketplace has become. Also think about that some industries are experiencing inherent hyper-growth. If you are the type of manager that reacts adversely to change or tries to throw his/her weight around and make Hispanic employees react with you, then you will encounter a tremendous amount of resistance that will be counter-productive to reaching your goals and objectives. Part of the transformation equation, needs to include performance measures for yourself as a manager.

- Communicate
- Keep people involved
- Get Hispanic Employees used to Constant Change and Continuous Improvement
- Contunually improve yourself

Benchmark "Top Performers"

Benchmark the top performers in your organization. Shadow them; find out what and how they are achieving their success! Get a description in writing, so this becomes a standard. These written descriptions of tasks and activities become your best practices. Then you translate these to others while continually improving them to the next level of productivity.

Use the +20/-20 Rule and the 1:3 Rule

You can avoid crisis management by becoming a proactive rather than a reactive manager. Part of being proactive is to give yourself and others a realistic timeline of deadlines and milestones.

The +20/-20 Rule says to add 20% more time to a project or deliverable that you are responsible for. In other words, if you think you can deliver the task on Thursday, you may want to give yourself until Friday. If you then think you'll be done by 9:00 a.m. on Friday, say 1:00 p.m. Practicing this method will allow you a comfort zone to complete tasks within the allotted time. The trick here is not procrastinating, knowing you have a comfortable "pad". By the same token, if someone owes you deliverable then take away 20%. If you need it Thursday at noon; you might want to tell them that you need it Thursday by 9:00 a.m., or even Wednesday by noon. You can always renegotiate.

Finally, the 1:3 rule says that for every minute, hour, etc that you invest in planning, giving direction, discussing etc., you will save 3 minutes, hours, etc., on the implementation side, so don't be afraid to invest time up front.

Creating Employee Development Plans:

Personal mission and vision statements are essential ingredients to performance standards and your organization's success. Sure, most organizations have their own mission and vision standards which become part of the enterprise fabric, but it's imperative to also have each department and individual create their own mission and vision statements that again feed into the overall plan.

This creates more solid ownership.

I remember an experience as a guest at the Ritz Carlton Hotel, Kapalua, Maui, Hawaii.
I was looking for the beach in order to participate in a teambuilding activity – also known as a volleyball game.

I was walking down this long walkway and arrived at a fork in the road with a sign that pointed to the beach in both directions. Not being familiar with the lay of the land I was pondering which direction to go, when I noticed some movement out of the corner of my eye. It was one of the gardeners who had put his rake down, and was briskly walking towards me. I distinctly remember his words, "How may I help you, sir?" It wasn't, "Can I help you, dude?", or "are you lost, man?"

I asked him for the volleyball courts and he proceeded to escort me towards the right beach. I asked him if he had just received customer service training and he told me, that his first few weeks on the property included an orientation which included providing service in the Ritz-Carleton way, escorting guests at least half-way to their destination. "Aha", I thought, but then he proceeded to tell me about his personal mission and vision statements. Now this was unique to hear so I asked him to elaborate on these:

His mission was to ensure that he exceeded his guest's expectations while they were in his designated areas. His vision was to have the most lush and well-manicured grounds on the property.

Did you catch it? These were his mission and vision statements, NOT anyone else's. He ended by telling me how he grew his own sod, which he used to repair the main lawns. When weeds were pulled from lawns, the holes were plugged with fresh sod, so no ugly holes show. WOW! Talk about job ownership!

Yeah, that's the Ritz, you may say, you pay a premium for that kind of service. Oh really, why can't we have this kind of service in our factories? The fact is that Hispanic employees have a deep desire to be of service, why not leverage this need?! You got to show them how...

Catch them doing "something right:"

All too often, it seems like some of us lay in wait for our employees to make a mistake. A mistake we knew they would eventually make. This attitude becomes a self-fulfilling prophecy. Why not turn the table and wait to catch Hispanic employees doing something right, and then you can reinforce this correct behavior?

"Liked Best - Next Time:"

This corrective assessment tool works great! I use it on my 12 year-old daughter and it works like a charm...

The concept behind it is that we eliminate critiques. You see, criticizing only creates temporary change in habits. Additionally you need to constantly monitor behavior. The saying says: Give a man a fish; he'll eat for one day. Teach him how to fish, and he'll eat for a lifetime.

This system will not only create independence, but will allow instant feedback, which opens dialogue answering the "why" behind it.

Here's How to Use It:

Let's say a Hispanic employee just completed a new task, you observed that he/she made several potentially costly or dangerous mistakes that you want to correct. The old style manager criticizes and yells, while belittling the Hispanic employee into submission. Two weeks later there's a worker's compensation claim...

The new manager asks the Hispanic employee over to talk.

What did you like best...?

You Say: "Listen, Juan, I want to talk to you about that process".
They Say: "OK"
You Say: "What did you like best about the way you handled yourself with....?" Or, you might say, "What did you like best about the way you did that...?"
They Say: "I think I did" .... They list all of the things they think they did right. However, they missed a few items you think need to be changed. You have a list in your head or in writing and you wait and see if they mention these.
You Say: "Is there anything else?" You want to toggle their brain for more information
They Say: "No" or mention a few more items. If they mention a few more items that happen to be on your list, then these are items you do not need to bring up, because they have told you that they are aware of them. Right?

Next Time...?

You Say: "What would you do differently Next Time?"   Now you are trying to shake out additional awareness items, encouraging more dialogue, while measuring their level of overall comprehension.
They Say: "Well, I found that I had to force the equipment, etc..."
You Say: "In addition to that, is there anything else?"   Now you are squeezing the proverbial "turnip" exhausting all avenues.

You listen, and you close with the following:

You Say: "I agree with your observations and comments. That's excellent. Have you thought about...?

Now you list all of the remaining observations or comments that you might have left on your list. It may be something like this:
You Say: "I agree with your observations and comments. That's excellent.

Have you thought about changing your hand position to reduce fatigue?

Have you thought about how you might place the raw materials closer to your workstation so you don't have to go so far to retrieve them or have to wait for them to be brought to you?

Have you thought about what you can be doing while you're waiting?

It is these kinds of questions, even if you have to go through an interpreter that will help the Hispanic employee discover new ways of increasing productivity. This is crucial to self-actualization and job ownership as well as increasing your productivity relative to your competition.

In the Olympics the difference between silver and a gold medal, is just a fraction of a second or millimeter. In business, having a leg up on the competition, even if it's just a little, goes a long, long way exponentially!

Let me illustrate:

Suppose your salesperson gives a 1% reduction in price. Would you consider this as significant? Come on, what's 1%? Let's take a look:

	No Discount	**1% Reduction in Price**
Sales	$100,000	$99,000
Cost of Goods Sold	$65,000	$65,000
Expenses	$30,000	$30,000
Income	$5,000	$4,000

The table above illustrates that even a 1% "insignificant" price reduction translates into a 20% reduction in your income. Would you consider 20% significant? I thought so.

When you show Hispanic employees this type of picture, and the reasoning behind it, (through a story and visuals) then it doesn't matter whether you're showing sales, tardiness, or waste.

Use effective Team rewards:

Rewards are effective if they take the entire team into consideration.   Imagine four Hispanic workers in the same department. Three of them work really hard, but the forth member is a socialite who spends his day cross-pollinating different departments. Suppose you implemented a reward that compensates the workers for achieving a goal. In this case they reach it. Everyone gets his or her reward, including the loafer. Does this seem fair?

Let's change the scenario where every team member must now reach a minimum level of performance. It doesn't matter if it's sales or manufacturing production. Let's say, the floor is 70% of overall goal, or plan. In order for people to get a reward, everyone, must reach at least the minimum! Do you think we will now have some peer pressure going? I guarantee it!

Make sure your rewards are based not only on reaching plan, but also on lowering losses, such as attrition, waste, costs, etc. Finally create the pool from Total Operating Expenses, this ensures that your "nut" and/or other obligations including administrative costs have been covered.

Understand the Growth Continuum:

This is the individual, or organization's maturity and experience level. For example a new Hispanic employee walks through your doors excited, and enthusiastic. Very highly motivated, but perhaps lacking the necessary skills or experience to do their job well.

After a period of time they know their job well, but are variably motivated due to human nature, an unchallenging position, negative work environment, etc.

There finally comes a time when the Hispanic employee takes on full ownership and accountability for their position and become self-motivated, and self-reliant. The continuum looks something like the following diagram:

Employee Unskilled or New	Employee Skilled at Their Job	Employee Excels at their job. Supervisory potential
High Motivation Low Skill	Variable Motivation Variable Competency	High Motivation High Competency
Your management style needs to be:	Your management style needs to be:	Your management style needs to be:
DIRECTIVE	**SUPPORTIVE**	**FACILITATIVE**
More "hands on" supplement with training & development.	"Back off!" Provide the tools to excel. Ask more, "tell" less…	Allow maximizing of talents & autonomy. Provide the tools to help them excel. Let them lead

CORRECT	BUILD	REINFORCE
Behavior	**Behavior**	**Behavior**
Give Specifics	"Really Liked*"	Give Specifics
Ask for Solutions	"Next Time"	Praise
		Challenge
(Assist in cognitive thinking)		

The closer to the left of this chart the Hispanic employee is, the more you direct and monitor and micromanage their behavior. The further to the right on the chart, the more autonomy you give.

Directing means: Telling, showing- what, when, how and soliciting & giving feedback.

A good way to direct is:

Tell – the Hispanic employee what you want them to do.

Show – them how it's done, when to do it, what good quality looks like

Practice – Have them practice in front of you, so you can observe them in action, and are able to make instant corrections.

Feedback- Get feedback. Ask, what they think, how it feels, How's it looks to them? (Neurolinguistics)

Monitor- Monitor continuously, or at regular intervals, or create a monitoring devise, such as a production report, which you or others can review periodically.

Be Specific:

Tell the Hispanic employee what specifically needs to be done, when it needs to be done, etc. Avoid the term "ASAP" because this means different things to different individuals. The

Hispanic employee will put everything else aside in a panic and the results will be less than optimal, and this is when mistakes happen. Give specific timelines so as not to confuse. Keep a follow-up log or record of these requested deadlines in a journal or your day planner. Follow-up by asking the Hispanic employee what questions they have for you, or to give you a status report or update of their progress towards goals.

Show the Hispanic employee how it's done; share shortcuts, best practices, provide picture job aides, etc. Pictures work best, because there may be a language barrier, and some of your Hispanic employees may be functionally illiterate.

Empower to implement consensus decisions.
Have the person practice in front of you. While they are going through the motions, you need to practice "magnet hips and magnet lips". In other words, keep your hands to yourself and shut up until the appropriate time for feedback is appropriate.

As a parent of small children myself, I have a tendency to try to do too much for my kids. Both children and employees need to be enabled to do things for themselves so that they can learn and grow and feel like they have accomplished something on their own. This is critical to raising self-esteem. Don't try to do it for them because you don't have the time to teach them or because you just want plain control. The rule of thumb is that for every hour you invest in teaching, showing, training, planning, etc. You save three (3) hours in the implementation. 1:3 Rule.

Remember that there is a feeling of persecution and low self-esteem issue with many Hispanics. Additionally some Hispanics have a tendency of not liking being told what to do. With this in mind, remember also that there exists a schizophrenic desire to be empowered. "Just don't tell me what to do". There's a fine balancing act you must perform in order to empower in an appropriate manner by showing and allowing mistakes to be made at this level so that you can correct the employee and contain the potential problem from growing here with the least amount of impact on the workflow or organization.

You'll want to get feedback on how they *felt* about the...whatever.

What they thought about the process and what they see. This is the practice of Neurolinguistics, utilizing all three senses.

Here's how you might ask: What did you think about that? How did it feel? Can you see how it (that) works? This establishes a powerful "anchoring" in reinforcing the new learned behavior.

Supporting Means:

Praising, listening, encouraging, and involving in decision making. Involvement in decision-making will be a challenge for the less educated Hispanic employees. The lower in assimilation level the closer to oppressive Theory "X" management styles they may have experienced. This modeled management style will then be the management style they think is the acceptable behavior. Additionally, many immigrants have been raised with the philosophy of "no es tu lugar"; it's not your place to say anything. In countries where Machismo and Theory "X" management still rule, the people are taught that it is not their place to say anything to the Patrón or Jefe. (The Boss)

So people mind their own business, are not heard from and play it safe. Speaking your mind in some countries may mean running the risk of getting shot or your entire family being killed, so it's best not to "rock the boat". Some countries are very oppressive, or don't function like they do in the U.S., so another feeling is one of "what's the use" or fatalistic.

I remember as a kid going to different theme parks and hearing my aunts and uncles comment at how impressed they were with how well-organized and efficient the lines for the rides or fast food was. I also remember hosting an exchange student from France who commented at how orderly and courteous Americans were standing in que (line) for everything. Apparently this is not the case in her country. The picture she painted was one of chaos and pandemonium anywhere near lines or traffic. Japanese friends tell me it's every man for himself boarding the bullet trains in Japan.

Facilitating means partnering with the Hispanic employee, and empowering them to take on an employee-leader role to move the process forward.

Empowering Means...

Giving authority.
Removing obstacles.
Establishing a suitable reward system.
The team is accountable for quality, cost, delivery, service levels, peer feedback, continuous improvement, planning & decision making!

Empowering employees also means empowering teams. Different types of Empowered Teams include:

Intra-functional

Employees as a group assume added responsibility for solving problems & making improvements within their departments.

Problem-Solving

Managers assign a problem to a temporary group of selected employees.

Cross-Functional

People from different functions or departments meet regularly to address mutual problems.

Self-Directed

Interactive Workgroups that handle daily operational issues with minimal supervision... Your primary goal is to Empower!

A collection of individuals who...

Are united around a common goal and objective.
Depend on each other to achieve goals!
Are structured to work together.
Share responsibility for some tasks.
Empowered to implement consensus decisions.

Below is an Employee Action Plan. Sit down with Hispanic employees to complete it together. Here's what you might say:
"I'd like for us to complete this action plan together. I would consider it a personal favor if you would commit to meeting and exceeding this plan. It's important to measure your own work so we can all become more successful. I will be asking everyone to complete one of these. (show you are not singling them out, or punishing them). Measuring performance will now become part of our regular business practices. I know you share the desire to work at (not for) a successful company, while also becoming successful yourself, right? I know you have the "ganas" (desire) that it takes to succeed."
This type of plan can also be applied to our families and our personal lives in helping us achieve our goals. This helps take us to the next level of excellence and success. Feel free to share this knowledge on "action-planning" with your

friends and relatives. I'd be happy to give you blank forms so you can take them home and show your family. Obviously, the business goals and objectives you and I establish for your job are confidential and I ask you to please not share these with anyone except your co-workers. You understand why, don't you? Fine. Let's get started:" (You want to walk them through their goals and objectives).

Prior to individual plans you have conducted a company-wide rollout meeting or informational general session in order to get everyone's buy-in. Perhaps you can't afford everyone off the floor, so you call people in groups (family). You state the reason for the meeting, sharing your goals and objectives, and your vision for where you want the company to go and the new way ion which everyone will be measured.
State clearly that no one has done anything wrong, or that you are NOT doing this to punish anyone. That you want everyone to create a culture of innovation, creativity, teamwork, self-reliance, and increased communication. Then you ask any of the following questions:

1. Why is it important to measure performance?
2. Why is it important to learn new ways?
3. Why is good communication important?
4. Why is working together important?
5. Why is reducing waste important?
6. Why is reducing mistakes, double-handling important?
7. Who's in charge? (Ultimately the answer is the customer!)

Finally, I suggest that you sit down with your direct reports once a quarter and agree on mutual goals and objectives that are based on your organization's goals and objectives.

This way you are developing employees and getting them on the "same page"... This makes it easier on you and improves your own delegation and multi-plexing skills.

Multi-tasking is completing multiple tasks at once.

Multi-plexing is completing or project managing multiple projects at once. In order to do this, you must use other people's talents and resources.

Below is an Employee Action Plan which you can use with your employees.

Employee Action Plan

I _____ commit to the
following Action Plan. I promise I will do my best
to improve in at least three areas over the next 90
days. Additionally, I commit to continuous and
consistent improvement thereafter.

Employee Signature: _____
Date: _____

Goals & Objectives for this Quarter	
Key Result Areas	PRIORITY (Percentage)
Goal #1 Goal #2 Goal #3	
Reasons Why I Need To Improve:	
Current Barriers & Obstacles:	

Specific Training or Skills Development Needed in Order To Reach my Goals & Objectives:

Improvement   Competence   Excellence

Strategic Alliances Needed In order To Achieve My Goals & Objectives:

Measure Each Quarter :	1Q / /	2Q / /	3Q / /	4Q / /
Improvement Areas: • • •				
Competence (Areas of adequate performance) • • •				

Self-Reliance (Areas of Excellence) • • •				

Plan de Acción Para Empleado

Yo _____me compromiso al próximo Plan de Acción. Prometo de hacer mi mejor esfuerzo para mejorarme en tres areas, por lo menos sobre los próximos 90 dias. Adicionalmente, me compromiso a mejoramiento continuo y consistente de alli en adelante.

Firma de Empleado:

_____

Fecha: _____

Metas y Objetivos Para Los Próximos Tres Meses	
Areas de Result ado	PRIORIDAD (Percentage)
Meta #1	
Meta #2	
Meta #3	
Razones Por que Debo de Cambiar	
Barreras y Obstáculos Corrientes:	

Entrenamiento Especifico o Adiestramento Necesario en orden de Lograr mis Metas y Objetivos. Areas de:

Mejoramiento   Capacidad   Excelencia

Alianzas Estrategicas Necesarias en orden Para Lograr mis Metas y Objetivos

Nombre de Empleado: _____

Fecha: _____

Medidas de Resultados	Primer Trimestre / /	Segundo Trimestre / /	Tercer Trimestre / /	Cuarto Trimestre / /
Fechas Para Lograr las Metas				
Deficiencia (Areas adonde actualmente necesito atención)				
Capacidad (Areas adonde tu tengo buena capacidad, pero adonde hay oportunidades para crecer y mejorar)				
Habilidades (Areas de Excelencia)				

You want to apply the Liked best, next time concept to your conversation as you review each of the areas, especially when you ask the Hispanic employee about the areas that he or she thinks they can improve upon. Be prepared for silence or to be told that everything is ok. Bide your time and show through your word and body language that together, you must come up with the information to complete this process. You might want to do it over two days, this way; they will have time to think about the areas of improvement, competency, and excellence. This will create ongoing dialogue and trust.

In closing, creating performance standards will help you in meeting your goals and objectives while motivating Hispanic employees. The forms in this chapter are designed and take into account the lowest level of education in the community.

You may have to make special accommodations for those Hispanic employees who may be functionally illiterate (don't read or write in their own language). Use an interpreter who is at supervisory level, not a coworker. Expect lots of questions. Be prepared to answer them from a personal (relationship) point-of-view, but with an organizational perspective. Celebrate successes and milestones, disperse power. Shift from being the boss to facilitating information and resources while empowering others.

Chapter 6

How To Manage & Motivate
The Different Levels of Hispanics

You have probably found that different levels of Hispanic employees exist within your organization. This acculturation, as it is called, is typical of the changing U.S. Hispanic workforce.

Each of the levels has different ethnicities, history, present world view(s), socio-economic class, learning style, gender and language preferences, among other traits, values and needs.

After hundreds of hours of research and personal observation in working with different levels of acculturated workers I will attempt to encapsulate each of the levels so that you may be better prepared to cope with, and effectively manage to each.

Immigrant
Level 1 –

Highly Motivated and optimistic, this type of individual sees the U.S. as the land of opportunity and may have traveled and travailed large distances to arrive to seek his or her fortune.

Reasons this person has left their motherland may include:

High levels of unemployment
Poor economic or volatile economic or political infrastructure, including freedom of speech or religious persecution. This person comes from a distinct class/caste system (Most Latin American countries have a very narrow or no middle-class, although some like Mexico and Brazil's are growing exponentially).

They arrive in the U.S. through relatives (trailblazers) already in the U.S.

Typical employee traits include:

Lack of formal or organized work experience.
Low or no education (zero to fourth grade is average, but there may be occasions where the individual has completed some higher education, and the language barrier is simply the determining factor).
More than likely does not speak English.
Relies on translator/Guides/Mentors
Employee has low or no technical, occupational, team skills

Does not recognize Quality. You must show and specify the reason(s) why.

Nationalism may cause on-the-job conflict

Does as told.

Doesn't deviate, ask questions or take initiative.

If they are asked questions, they will rely on the friend or relative that referred him/her to the job (their guide) for the answers.

Can work independently given the right situation: Give clear instructions, and simple tasks.

Use photographs or pictures to get your point across the language and potential illiteracy barrier.

Prefers hand tools to machinery. So you have to formally train on fully utilizing power tools and automation.

First Generation & Consecutive Generation – Foreign-born

Level 2

Variable Motivation

Some work experience

Low or no education. 4th grade to 8th. Very few with high school degrees.

Speaks vocational English (at best)

Riverts to Spanish dominant

May or may not need translator depending on how long they have been in the U.S.

May or may not need Spanish-speaking Guide/Mentor depending on whether they have consciously decided to let go of the "training wheels". You job is to create a culture that encourages independence.

Some fear of discrimination.

Some Basic technical or occupational skills.

Does not recognize quality. Show what and why of quality.

Help them get over the fact that they are there as a resource for the organization to make a profit.

Nationalism may cause on-the-job conflict.

Works as told.

Ventures out to ask other Hispanic employees he/she trusts: compadres and comadres.

May work independently given their previous work-experience.

Needs clear instructions and clear understanding of task outcome.

Favors hand tools to machinery, or automation.

First Generation & Consecutive Generation – U.S.-born Spanish Dominant
Level 3
Variable Motivation

More work experience

Low or no education.

46% of U.S. Latinos, approximately 15 million DO NOT have a High School degree. Going to work and becoming caretakers are two biggest reasons.

Some High School or High School equivalent (GED)

More than likely has attended company-sponsored workforce development classes.

Speaks English, prefers Spanish or Spanglish

Prefers speaking Spanish at.

May or may not have sensed/experienced some discrimination.

Recognizes Quality when well defined. Provide QC and accountability training.

Nationalism may cause on-the-job conflict; there may be some hostility towards immigrants.

Works as told.

Ventures out to ask other Hispanic employees he/she trusts.

Has close-knit clique.

Could be in leadership position, but needs lots of encouragement.

If in leadership position will be ultra-conservative in decision-making.

Micro manages co-workers or direct reports so they won't look bad.

Can work independently relying on their previous work-experience.

Needs a clear, reliable instruction for task outcome.

Will become de-motivated if process or systems are not predictable, or if management lacks direction.

Favors hand tools to machinery or riverts to "old ways" under pressure.

Will add more people rather than look at process improvements.

Has trouble delegating.

Can fully utilize machinery, or automated process if given the proper training.

Second & Consecutive Generation – U.S.-born English Dominant/Spanish Preference
Level 4
High Motivation

Understands & works well in teams

May have attended company-sponsored workforce development classes and is utilizing the techniques.

Has attended seminars outside of workplace.

Prefers speaking English at work (may or may not have accent).

Prefers speaking Spanish at home can handle workplace conflicts effectively.

Some education, usually High School, or GED (high school equivalency), or technical certificate.

Speaks English, prefers Spanish or Spanglish.

(May or may not have "barrio" accent)

Culturally Hispanic.

Speaks English at work, may speak Spanish to other Spanish-Speaking employees.

Prefers speaking Spanish at work.

May or may not have sensed or experienced some discrimination, but may need coaching in effectively following policies and procedures and getting others to "buy in" without taking it personally.

Recognizes Quality when well defined.

Needs your assistance in taking on job responsibility and accountability. Provide QC capability

Nationalism may not be as big an issue on-the-job, but there may be some hostility towards immigrants and nationalistic bickering (if it exists).

Works as told. May be reticent about taking initiative.

Has a good, established relationship with other Hispanic employees he/she trusts.

Has close-knit clique of compadres or comadres

Perhaps is acting in leadership role officially or unofficially.

Second & Consecutive Generation – U.S.-born English Dominant/English Preference
Level 5
High Motivation

Understands & works well in teams.
May have attended company-sponsored workforce development classes and is utilizing the techniques regularly.
Actively seeks out more information.
Attends seminars outside of workplace regularly.
Prefers speaking English at work (may or may not have accent).
Prefers speaking English at home can handle workplace conflicts effectively.
Solid education, High School degree, or GED certificate (high school equivalency) and AA degree or higher.

- 6% of U.S. Latinos earn Associate degrees
- 3% earn Master's degrees
- 2.3% earn Doctorate degrees

Speaks broken or rudimentary Spanish or no Spanish at all.
May not speak Spanish, or speaks "Spanglish"
Prefers English at work and at home.
May speak with English accent when speaking Spanish to Spanish-dominant people.
Bi-cultural or culturally American. Hispanic by heritage.

Most likely does <u>not</u> have a "barrio" accent, or accent is hardly detectable.

Recognizes Quality consistently, but needs your empowerment in taking job ownership. Provide QC capability, and clear parameters or scope of authority.

May be vocal to initiate change.

Nationalism may not be as big an issue on-the-job, no hostility towards immigrants. Empathizes with others.

Self-starter. Demonstrates good initiative. Has good established relationships with other mainstream employees he/she trusts.

May be ambivalent about discrimination, or gets frustrated or impatient about the discrimination "issue".

Strives for Quality when measured.

More than likely in official leadership role

Can work very independently. You may still need to train on the importance of interdepartmental interdependence.

Needs clear, reliable goals and objectives for task outcome.

Will become de-motivated if process or management lacks direction or organization, or if they feel underutilized or slighted.

Favors automation, autonomation and streamlined process controls.

Understands & works well in teams and can delegate well.

Chapter 7

Effective Leadership

It is extremely important to model appropriate leadership behavior to the Hispanic community. You are under the microscope in many more ways than you might think, and any deviation or faltering on your part will "taint" or undermine your authority. Like it or not, you are viewed as a representative of the particular ethnic group you represent and your behavior will be interpreted as a broad-brush trait of this ethnicity. Additionally, any breaches may heavily undermine the inter-cultural trust factor (confianza) which is so important within the community.

With this in mind, I want to share 18 winning Leadership Strategies every Business Owner, Manager or Supervisor Needs to Succeed with Hispanic employees:

1. Leadership - Determine the best leadership style to use in different circumstances:
   Directing, Supporting, Developing, and Facilitating. The more independent the
   Hispanic employee, the more to the facilitating-end of the spectrum your style should become.

2. Communication - Enhance your working relationships with your Family, Employees,

Boss, co-workers and others.   Listen proactively.
Build inter-cultural bridges.

3. Problem Solving - Master the 6-Step Problem-
   Solving Model (Chapter 10).   Learn scientific
   methods, and teach specific methods for
   problem solving such as:

   Force field, Cause & Effect, and Root Cause
   Analysis. Ishikawa (fishbone analysis),
   Pareto and Gantt Analysis, etc

4. Decision-Making - Overcome "analysis
   paralysis". Do it now, but involve Hispanic
   employees.

5. Goal-Setting - Craft a Mission Statement for
   your department or company that makes
   your priorities clear to everyone. Involve
   Hispanic employees in creating
   departmental mission and vision statements.
   Create a personal mission & vision
   statement. Have employees create personal
   mission and visions statements. Remind
   Hispanic employees that these principles will
   apply to the betterment of their
   Families, and show "how".

6. Team-Building - Multiply the efforts of your staff by unleashing team power! Create the "family" team!

   Together
   Everyone
   Achieves
   More.

7. Delegation - Delegate if someone can do it, better, faster, less expensive, or if it helps in another's personal development.

8. Coaching - Discover how developing "one-on-one" relationships with Hispanic employees can dramatically improve productivity! There's no such thing as a dumb employee, only a dumb boss does not develop the employee to their full potential!

9. Morale Management - Keep spirits high despite a hyper-changing work environment.

10. Time & Stress Management - Uncover hidden pockets of time in your day. Be effective and efficient. Concentrate on what's important vs. "urgent". Stay focused!

11. Conducting Effective Meetings - Learn the art of "facilitating" meetings that really get results. Share-leadership, respect other's time – and stick to an agenda, there are no "dumb" questions. Encourage participation, know the different types of

meetings: Planning, strategic, decision-making, training, information, etc. Use the "parking Lot" technique to keep meetings on track. Evaluate the meeting each time for effectiveness.

12. Performance Planning – Concentrate on filling your positions using competency-based factors, rather than job descriptions. Conduct evaluation and improvement Sessions at least Quarterly. Tie individual goals and objectives to the enterprise goals and objectives.

13. Interviewing - Use experiential questions to make sure you hire the right people for the job!

14. Disciplinary Actions and Termination – Handle difficult situations professionally. Know when and where to seek assistance when you're in over your head.

15. Legal Issues - Know the law when it comes to hiring and firing, and workplace conduct.

16. Lose the "E" in EGO to get "GO."!
    Lose the   "E" in "emotion to get "motion"!

17. Let go! -- Empower Hispanics! Start with the
    assumption that most people want to
    do the right thing. No matter what the
    strategy, initiative, change, product or
    program. Answer the following questions:

- How is the change relevant to what they do?
- What specifically do you want them to do?
- How will they be measured and what consequences will they face?
- What tools and support will you make available?
- What's in it for them?

18. Give of yourself freely! Givers gain.

You may want to start off by doing a little SWOT
analysis on yourself to leverage your strong points
and shore-up your weaknesses. As you develop
strengths they will lead you to more
opportunities. Any weaknesses left unchecked --
lead to threats!

Strengths:

Weaknesses

Opportunities

Threats

Motivating and managing Hispanic employees is a continuing process. The lower the education and assimilation level the more you will have to mentor and develop. Below you will find a couple of tables I have developed to help you effectively guide and create more self-reliant and productive Hispanic employees.

The forms are designed for you to sit down with the employee ahead of time to identify, clarify and agree on an action plan for attainment of goals.

The first column let's you identify and mutually agree on the priority.

The second column tells the Hispanic employee the weight of the priority. You can specifically tell them that you want them to spend 60% of their time on the first priority (A), 20% on the second priority (B) and another 20% on the third priority (C).

So in an 7-hour day (8 hours minus half-hour for lunch and two 15-minute breaks) 4.2 hours would be invested on Priority A, and 1.4 hours on priority B and C respectively.

Some folks work longer hours, so the math may vary.

You attach a value to the priorities in the third column.

It's good to attach a minimum attainment requirement, say 70% of goal, whatever the goal.

If your employees are on a bonus system this
would equate as follows:

70%	80%	90%	100%	120%
$25	$50	$60	$70	$100

This concept also works well if your company
does not provide an employee bonus. What you
do then, is equate the attainment of goals to roll
up into your annual review and merit increases.
You can track on a quarterly basis and get an
average for each quarter.

Then when it comes to the annual review you
have solid documentation which can justify the
merit increase given.

This system is great because it takes both the
guesswork and the subjectivity out of the
equation. Employees cannot claim discrimination
or favoritism. Here's how the merit increase
would work given a range of 3%-6%.

70% 120%	80%	90%	100%
3% 8%	4%	5%	6%

At review time you review your employees
quarterly performance. You have documented
their actual performance and take an average of
the quarters. If they averaged 80% of their goals,
then it's obvious what merit increase they have

earned. What if the average is 85%? Then use
regular math rounding principles. 5 or below
rounds down, 6 or above rounds up. No
exceptions and every manager does it the same.

You'll notice that in both cases I included a 120
percentile.
My philosophy is that you want to make it VERY
ATTRACTIVE for any performance over 100%!
You may want to include additional percentiles
above 100%. At one company, we included a 200
percentile, and we had extremely motivated
employees.

Work the numbers backwards. What does your
organization get in return for rewarding 100%
plus? Secondly, make sure that even the 100% is
attainable, or you'll have frustrated employees.

**Track Employee Quarterly goals and
objectives:**

Priority	Percentage Weight	Value
What Strategy will you use? What Tactics will you use to develop your strategy?	What percentage of your time will be devoted towards attaining this goal?	Place a value on the goal as a reward? Set a minimum performance standard? I.e. 70%= $700, 80% =$800, 90% = $900,etc.

List your **Strategy** (How will you attain it?) **Tactics** (What methods will you use)		
Strategy **Tactics**		

Part of motivating and managing Hispanic employees is the effective use of modeling the behaviors that you want or providing the tools that would ensure their success.   This is extremely important with the less educated or less assimilated employees.

Employee Task & Activity Determination

Key Result Areas

Are areas you want the
Hispanic employee to
focus on. In order of priority:

Goal #1

Goal #2

Goal #3

PRIORITY Percentage

Explain percentage of their time you want them working on the specific Key Result Areas above and why it is important.

Example: it will make your job easier, more effective.   It will help us garner more market share.   It will help us increase our profits, etc. it's ok to talk about profit, *Ganancias* the Hispanic employee will understand and appreciate your honesty.

Identify Current Hurdles, Obstacles, or Barriers

This is an area you want to have good dialogue so you can separate the perceived from the real barriers. Get specifics as to why the Hispanic employee feels about a certain situation. You have to get past their heart to get to their soul, and their mind.

Ask about specific training or skill development needed in order to reach goals & objectives: Be prepared to give the needed developmental support.

Define the specific Tasks and Activities you want them to focus on. Here's an example of what a traditional job description might look like for a tele-marketer compared to a task and activity profile.

Traditional Job Description: Telemarketer

Responsible for making outbound sales and marketing calls.

Now compare the more specific and <u>measurable</u> task and activities for each level of competence:

Telemarketer: Minimal/Apprentice level

Identify target zip codes, order database, rehearse script, deliver script with maximum of 5 "burps" per presentation, utilize answers to objections screen, review product and sales literature, operate computer and headset, understand predictive dialing, understand sales quota, and produce at 70% level within 2 months of hiring.

Telemarketer: Competent Level

Identify target zip codes, order database, rehearse script, deliver script with maximum of 3 "burps" per presentation, utilize answers to objections screen, be able to effectively answer the three most common objections consistently, review product and sales literature, operate computer and headset, understand predictive dialing, understand sales quota, produce at 80% level 10 out of 12 months.

Telemarketer: Proficient/Expert level

Identify target zip codes, order database, rehearse script, deliver script with maximum of 1 "burp" per presentation, have answers to objections memorized and utilize effectively, review product and sales literature, operate computer and headset, understand predictive dialing, assist in loading of database, understand sales quota, produce at 90% level 10 out of 12 months. Will be put on disciplinary action plan if misses 90% two-months in a row.

I think you'll agree that the tasks and activities are much clearer to the Hispanic employee in knowing what to do and what is expected. This system eliminates guessing, discrimination or favoritism.

In closing, I urge you to practice the concept of Kaizen

This is the Japanese philosophy of continuous and consistent improvement.

Share this philosophy with Hispanic employees so that they understand the continual changes that are required and occurring in today's fast-paced business climate.

Chapter 8

Performance Management: Sustaining A New Culture of Continuous Improvement

In the previous chapter we talked about the opportunity and responsibility for you, the manager to continually observe the performance of each Hispanic employee and communicate regularly on that performance. Because development is interdependent rather than independent, you must adopt a dual focus.

First, as the manager you must observe and provide feedback for performance in order to promote ongoing growth and development, this is critical with Hispanic employees, as most will not have the necessary education and skill sets, depending on their assimilation level. Many recent immigrants may even be functionally illiterate.

Secondly, you must focus on continuous development in order to achieve maximum performance and productivity. Your organization must encourage total cultural acceptance of these concepts at all levels. I've seen organizations with great potential die because the owners or executive management merely play lip service to a new way of thinking, and revert to the old way of doing things as soon as the consultant leaves.

As a supervisor or manager, you must essentially take on the role of coach and "champion" for this new movement. Get as many other individuals committed, from all levels, so you can establish a critical mass that drives this continuous improvement forward.

As the coach you need to assess your line-up of employees to determine each of their developmental levels, so that you can coach them accordingly. For example, you will probably need to be more "hands on" with a new employee than with a more experienced, self-reliant employee that performs at the top of his or her level.

One pitfall to watch out for is to assume that a tenured employee is self-reliant. Tenured employees must also adapt to the new ways, and you must get them involved and on your side in a proactive manner. If you don't do this, you may get sideswiped later.

Observation: A new employee gets used the speed, or pace of work because they don't know any different. A tenured employee may complain about this new pace and resist it creating conflict.

You need to recognize that performance rarely exceeds the tools and process that are being applied, so you need to observe, provide feedback and establish a systematic approach to improving new skills, knowledge, effort and activity, that feeds into your organization's goals and objectives. (Enterprise goals & objectives)

Performance occurs along a spectrum. There are two points to watch as you develop Hispanic employees. I call these points, transitionary points: One   point   is   where   competent performance drops to the deficient level; the other point to watch and monitor is at the point where competent performance moves up to proficient.

You want to encourage, or support employee growth up and watch, monitor, or correct employee backsliding. This will assist you in creating a highly productive workplace. Assisting Hispanic employees with job ownership while implementing quality at their level is called quality at the source.

Hispanic Employee Growth Spectrum

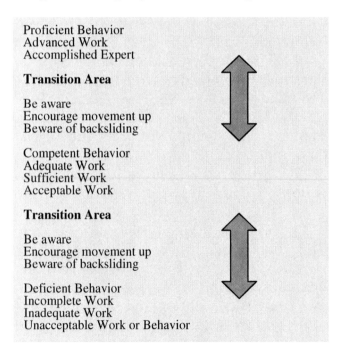

Proficient Behavior
Advanced Work
Accomplished Expert

Transition Area

Be aware
Encourage movement up
Beware of backsliding

Competent Behavior
Adequate Work
Sufficient Work
Acceptable Work

Transition Area

Be aware
Encourage movement up
Beware of backsliding

Deficient Behavior
Incomplete Work
Inadequate Work
Unacceptable Work or Behavior

There are two aspects to employee development and skill building.

First, is competence. This is the knowledge and skills the individual brings to a specific goal or task. This is why you must first assess your Hispanic employees. Write it down. Keep a log of classes attended and their progress. If bases are loaded, you as the coach must rely on the skills of the "pinch-hitter" to bring in the runs, right?

Second, is commitment. This is the individual's motivation and confidence on that goal or task. This level of commitment rises exponentially as you develop your relationships with Hispanic employees. Hispanic employees will have more *confianza*, or confidence and loyalty towards you.

There are basically two management styles to adopt as you take Hispanic employees up through their developmental growth spectrum:

Directing-Telling and showing employees what to do, when to do it, how to do it and providing frequent feedback on results.

Supporting-Praising, listening, encouraging and involving employees in decision-making.

The table below illustrates that you can develop Hispanic employees by utilizing a combination of these management styles.

C. High Supportive Low Directive	**B. High Directive High Supportive**
Provide tools for skills development while involving Hispanic employee will begin to create self-managed employees Not as much resistance or time needed here. Systematic, reliable systems and processes are crucial!	You'll encounter the most challenge and resistance going from A to B. Hispanic employees have begun to "get it" and have experienced some success and autonomy.
D. Low Supportive Low Directive	**A. High Directive Low Supportive**
When systematic & reliable systems and processes are in place, along with well-developed employees, you become facilitator of information. Employee becomes knowledge source. Use this self-reliant individual to teach others.	New Hispanic employees or low-skill levels need lots of "hands on". You begin to mold continuous change in your company and worker culture. Train, train, train: provide visual job aides. (lots of pictures) Use "buddy system", especially if there's a language barrier. Hire bilingual, bicultural instructors. Learn to speak Spanish.

You will encounter the most resistance from Hispanic employees going from A to B. They do not yet believe or understand.

 Resistance will begin to level off as Hispanic employees begin to understand and begin experiencing Some successes.

 Resistance is diminished as Hispanic employees really believe and embrace this new empowerment.

Part of continuous improvement is continuous feedback as you develop Hispanic employees from one level to the next. Remember the Hispanic employee may be overly sensitive to "criticism" and may take it as a discriminatory, so your feedback sessions need to remain positive. Stay away from the word "critique". Instead use words like:

- Measurement
- Assessment
- Milestone
- Development

Use the "liked best, Next Time" technique described earlier in the text.

Note: Training creates dependency, development creates self-sufficiency.

Now it's now time to switch to a more "focused" approach to reinforce the desired behaviors. You therefore, need to provide a tool for continued improvement. With this in mind, I have prepared the Coaching Action Plan below for you to use in getting commitment from your employees.

Coaching Action Plan:

1.   Write/Escriba:

Your Organization's Mission Statement/Misión de la compañia:

_____

Your Department's Mission/Misión de tu departamento:

_____

Your Personal Work Mission Statement/Tu propia misión para tu trabajo. What is your life mission?
Cual es tu misión par tu vida?

(Ala Ritz Carlton story...)

_____

_____

Once you have identified the above, then you can move on to sitting down with your employees and creating their "buy in" through an Employee Action Plan. The employee action plan feeds into the above. This leaves no doubt in anyone's mind as to what priorities, goals and objectives are agreed on.

Step 1: Sit down with your employees.

Step 2: Remember to use the "Like Best", "Next Time" approach to discuss areas of current competency and areas where improvements are needed.

Step 3: Together develop an Action Plan. Include milestones and deadlines.

Step 4: Review what skills and tools are needed for the improvement.
          Provide those tools.

Hispanic employees need to be aware of what is expected. Many Hispanic hourly employees only look at "working hard". So we need to develop them in an appropriate manner. Remember, individuals develop at different rates and at different levels of skill... Part of this developmental process is to assist each Hispanic employee grow in areas of deficiency and reinforce developing areas of competence and excellence.

Chapter 9

Teaching & Creating a Quality-driven Workplace

Quality improvement with Hispanic employees begins by making this concept part of your organization's cultural change and part of the Hispanic employee's new frame of reference. Typically managers have related quality to standards and measurements and work schedules and have succinctly expressed this to Hispanic employees. "Do it right the first time" is a catch all phrase that's similar to "do it as soon as possible" Both of these phrases are too broad and are not specific enough to effectuate change.

Quality is defined as meeting or exceeding the needs and expectation of the customer.

Thus, one of your major goals is to determine what the customer wants and then fine-tune your process and procedures to ensure they get it. Robert Demming's teachings embraced several techniques and methodologies for process control, but they also embraced the philosophy that quality is the responsibility of everyone in the organization. Quality at the Source. The Japanese adopted his ideas, during the 1950's and over time refined them. They extended the application of process improvement from manufacturing to administrative functions and service industries so that the quality concept affected the whole organization. Japanese industry succeeded in taking over many markets because they were able to drive down their costs while at the same time improving the quality of their products. A big portion of cost reduction had to do with eliminating waste and low value activities.

In 1926 Henry Ford said, "One of the most noteworthy accomplishments in keeping the price of Ford products low is the gradual shortening o f the production cycle. The longer an article is in the process of manufacture and the more it is moved about, the greater is the ultimate value".

As we have mentioned in Chapter 1 and 2 many of the traits, needs and values of Hispanic employees would need to be modified in order to help with true quality implementation. Six words will enable you to initiate new behavioral and attitudinal changes:

- Employee Motivation
- Measurements
- Rewards
- Waste Reduction

Motivation for Hispanic employees in your organization will come from relational or people skills as well as the level of commitment to Hispanic needs in the organization.

What This means To You:
The way you speak to Hispanic employees, the level of respect for the individual and the culture, and other benefits and programs, even the way your organization communicates strategic or company-wide developments will motivate the Hispanic employee. Of course, opportunity for skill development and advancement in promoting Hispanics (male and female) to key management positions shows that your organization recognizes the importance and worth of the Hispanic employee. Because of our previous discussion of low education levels in the Hispanic community, it is critical that you offer continuous educational opportunities and mentorship programs inside and outside the company in order to groom and attract other Hispanic employees.

 Unfortunately many companies still treat their employees like mushrooms: keeping them in the dark and feeding them manure. "It's too much of a hassle or it's too costly" to implement these programs with "these people" or to try to communicate on a quarterly basis the company's goals and objectives. What I call a "state-of-the company" address.

Even public company's I've consulted with look at me cross-eyed when I mention this reporting concept. Sometimes they tell me that employees could go to the web to search for the company's 10-Q report, or they could go to their stockbroker to find out. These two comments tell me clearly that management has no clue about the Hispanic demographics. Obviously, these are companies that still have a few things to learn about the Hispanic market. In my opinion your organization will have more motivated Hispanic employees when financial, sales and marketing, product development customer service or whatever information you have available is shared with the entire organization. If you are familiar with Open Book Management then you know that this concept aims at bringing decision-making and accountability to the lowest level in the organization: its Employees! And Hispanic employees want to know where the competition "ate their lunch" and where they excelled. When you understand this, then you are able to tap into another basic value of competition within the Hispanic community. When you ignore or fail to direct this competition within your organization, then this is when you get negative competition, which causes conflict in your workplace.

You need to clearly explain how what they do on a day-to-day basis affects "the bottom line". This type of disclosure should be your regular fiduciary responsibility. Your organization can utilize this type of employee knowledge to improve customer service, products and services, reduce scrap, and have better teams, more effective meetings, and much more. I remember when I worked at Blue Cross of California. Every quarter Leonard Schaeffer, the President and CEO of this multi-billion dollar organization would make his rounds out to the satellite facilities along with other senior executives to provide us with the quarterly report. Talk about accountability and motivation! It was excellent. There was always time for a question and answer period and all management was approachable, and available.

A word of caution: Don't assume all of your Hispanic employees come from low educational levels. You need to assess the individual levels of education and experience and offer different "career tracks". You don't want to frustrate or cubbyhole a fast learner in a class that teaches down to them. Additionally, I've seen many well-intentioned consultants and instructors teach down to low education level employees, or functionally illiterate employees. Don't do this. Teach up! Challenge! S T R E T C H Hispanic employees! Make the lessons culturally relevant! You will be pleasantly surprised.

Here are some ideas on culturally relevance:

In a Vocational English as a Second Language (VESL) class,   rather than concentrate on the often tedious and elementary English texts. "How are you today, fine...?" I have the class take a break from traditional grammar by reading English articles from Hispanic magazines or organizations. The students read these articles out loud to each other. Then, I have them translate the text. They ask questions and we review those words or phrases that give them difficulty. We create a spelling list from these words and test on these later. The most recent article read in class was one on AIDS in the Barrio. Do you think the class paid attention? You bet!

Here are a few other technique I use to increase the effectiveness of knowledge transfer.

Peer Group- I use this technique as positive "pressure" to succeed.   After assessing the capability of the different Hispanic employees, this is a good way to facilitate partnerships between Hispanic employees.   This type of collaboration will be new for most Hispanic employees because of the pervasive "nationalism" and sub-segmentation that exists within the community.   During class session, I group the employees in groups with skill levels that are as close to being balanced as possible.   I have assigned the Hispanic employee with the most capability to be the team captain, or assistant, so to speak.

I am able to "clone" myself this way and transfer the learning more effectively.   Sometimes you can't do it all yourself, so you are spreading the load.

The concept is introduced and then the information is reinforced by the team captain first by the instructor, then by the team captain in each group.   Remember that one of the basic tenants of the Hispanic community is "family", so this consultative approach works very well.   Don't be concerned if they all begin talking at once. This is normal behavior.

You can take this concept up a notch; by training these team captains ahead of time and having well-prepared materials.   Then the knowledge gets transferred at a higher level of competence, it's sort of a train-the-trainer.

Partnering with Key Employees- This technique mixes in key people that the Hispanic employees will need to work with effectively. Sometimes the language, or misperceptions cause communication and collaboration breakdowns. We all know that people are interdependent of each other, rather than independent... in needed to support the use of the training on the job.

Déjà vu - This technique is similar to repeating television commercials. Have you ever been watching your favorite TV? Show and there's a luxury car or SUV commercial. Then the next commercial comes on, AND THEN previous luxury car or SUV commercial comes on again. What happens? You generally sit up, pay more attention and ponder on why this commercial is repeating. Well, I use this same technique with spelling. I'll have the Hispanic employees take the test. We'll grade the test together. Then I'll have them immediately take the test again. The retention and the learning are increased tremendously. An alternative is to "pop" the exact same test somewhere during the course of the days' session. People stay alert and they get immediate feedback through this auto-analysis.

Pictures Instead of Words – Remember that many of Hispanics may have a low education or be functionally illiterate, not capable of reading or writing in their mother tongue. It's therefore, very important to use lots of graphics, diagrams in your presentation. Research has shown that it's also easier for us to remember pictures when we can attach a picture to it. To remember Walter's name for example, you might want to remember a watermelon floating over his head. For Rita, a dancing señorita. Got it? Good.

Digging for gold – Invariably there will be material presented during the class session that will elicit blank stares or questions. After discussing the material more in depth while it's fresh on everyone's mind, you can then "flag" this material and present it in a different manner the next time around. This reinforces the material.

Knowledge and cognition. One of the hallmark achievements of cognitive science is the confirmation of the dual nature of cognition: all human intellectual activities, such as thinking, communicating, problem solving, and learning require both processes and knowledge. This is important because it points out the near futility of attempting to improve cognitive ability simply by improving "processes" such as "reading," "writing," "critical thinking," and so forth without recognizing that high levels of ability in performing these processes requires high levels of knowledge on which the processes can operated. What this means to you is that providing an intervention or applicable method to reinforce the training is critical to long-term behavioral changes.

On-the-job use of this learning has to be part of the process.

I do some work for the California Department of
Trade and Commerce and they call this
intervention Structured On-Site Training, or
SOST. The philosophy is that in order to
maximize the effectiveness of the week's
classroom session I spend the following week
working the previous week's theory in an
applicable way with the Hispanic employee.

Rather than theoretical case studies, it's a good
idea to divide the classes into task teams that
address actual issues and concerns at your
company. Then you get to work on utilizing the
classroom techniques in tackling the situation.
Hispanic employee's experiences the learning
therefore comprehend and retain this knowledge
longer.

This doesn't mean that you will begin to instantly
see a dramatic difference in production in all
cases. What it does mean is that as long as you
continue with consistent employee development,
then you will see incremental increases that
cumulatively will have a very significant positive
impact. In the early 90's the National Adult
Literacy Survey (NALS) conducted a study of
literacy skills for U.S. adults aged 16 to over 65.
The study used prose, document and quantitative
scales to measure literacy. The scale ranged from
0 to 500. The scores were reported using scale
scores for each of the three different types of
literacy measured (task domains). Both people
and tasks (items) were given scales cores. For
instance, a person with a skill level of 210 would
have a probability of 80 percent of performing a

task that had a difficulty level of 210. However, other people with lower skill levels of 150 only had a 32 percent probability of being able to perform the same 210 level task. People at a 200 level had a 74 percent probability of performing the same level 210 level task, and people at a 300 skill level had a 99 percent probability of performing the same level 210 task. The study did not take ethnicity into account directly. I mention this because the study took into account incarcerated adults, which might reflect a higher minority population. This study is critical in substantiating the importance of going from a job description to a task and activity description in order to measure proficiency.

The study divided the adults into five skill levels:

Level 1: 0-225
Level 2: 226-275
Level 3: 276-325
Level 4: 326-375
Level 5: 376-500

We can translate this concept to the Hispanic community and the different educational and skill levels within the community to establish minimums and maximum levels of proficiency in order to understand that Hispanic employees with lower skill levels will be able to perform certain specified tasks previously out of their reach, but at a lower attainment level. So you have to keep reinforcing in order to keep the growth continuum growing. The study supports the continual need to develop proficiency-based work. Additionally, this is why a selection process that measures previous experience or the likelihood of certain attributes is an invaluable tool to your overall success.

This is why utilizing creative techniques opens up the Hispanic mind to get you closer to the higher skill levels so that Hispanic employees will move up the percent of probability in performing certain tasks. By understanding this now, hopefully your frustration level will diminish somewhat because your expectations will now be more in line with the appropriate level of Hispanic employee skill attainment. This is especially important when you consider the type of education that many U.S. Hispanics receive. In the United States, 48% of Hispanics receive an inner-city education. In his famous essay, The Seven-Lesson schoolteacher (New Society Publishers 1992) John Taylor Gatto talks about how schools create intellectual dependency. "Good students wait for a teacher to tell them what to do." Conformity triumphs, while curiosity has no place of importance. He goes on to relate some horrific experiences as a substitute teacher in York City where he ran into some genuinely horrifying experiences with school kids being denied basic tools in the belief that there are some things these kids couldn't do. I call this the "dumbing down" of the curriculum.

STRETCH Hispanic employees. They will pleasantly surprise you. Think about this: Hispanic employees are survivors. They are able to migrate thousands of miles to a new land with a different language and customs to create a new life. I challenge you the supervisor or manager, in creating a new life for them at work also. A life of inclusiveness, understanding and continual achievement.

Chapter 10

Effective Problem Solving

Effective problem solving is a key to creating more self-reliant and exceptional Hispanic employee. I cannot stress the importance of realizing that many of the values, needs, and current approaches within the Hispanic community may create some roadblocks towards effective problem solving at your company.

In an earlier chapter, we mentioned that the different needs and values may even create negative and destructive conflict which may further hinder the progress that you want.

Remember that you want positive conflict, which creates innovation and progress.

An example of negative conflict would be:

Hispanics from different nationalities seem to sabotage each other's efforts at every turn. There is strife, gossip and continual bickering.

An example of positive conflict:

Hispanics from different nationalities have been working effectively as a team. They come to you as a group reporting that the Quality Control Department is not communicating well with them, rejects their work without explanation, and does not allow them to view the blueprints without a lot of "red tape".

Why is this conflict good? Because it shows that this group is working cohesively. That they have good intentions regarding a common goal, the quality of the work, and increasing intradepartmental communications and fostering self-reliance by gaining access to important information.

Your job would then be to assist this group in effective problem solving to see if this is a true and accurate state of affairs, and to resolve this situation on their own by following a systematic approach to pinpoint potential causes, effects and the impact to the organization.

It's very tempting for you to bulldoze your way through this, kicking down doors, barking orders, directing people, getting other management involved, etc. And you might be successful in meeting your super-tight deadlines, but you have just taught your crew that bullying gets the job done and that you are "the hero" that can solve all of their future problems. Now you have a problem...

Let's take a look at a very simple systematic approach called the Six-Step Problem Solving Model.

The first step in this model is to define the problem.

The word "problem" (problema) in the Hispanic culture is a very negative term, and you will find Hispanic employees may get immobilized at the mere thought of approaching a daunting "problema".

This model is effective because it teaches people to remain calm in the face of a storm. Just like in martial arts. The Sensei or teacher teaches his students to remain calm when attacked.
This way, you are relaxed and can quickly switch to punch, counter-attack mode. If one were to tense up when attacked,

one would first have to relax, then punch, then counter-attack.   Eliminating this extra step and additional split-second could may the difference between life and death.

Now, I'm not advocating violence.   What I am advocating is arming Hispanic employees with the concept of thinking before acting.   You see our culture has been taught to work hard, and we're excellent workers.   We haven't been taught to work smart.   That's where you come in.   You may already have witnessed that we can be very clever, and very resourceful, so when you redirect these very positive qualities you will be able to accomplish your goals and objectives!

When confronted by a problem here's what you tell, Juan, or Maria: "Juan, here's what I want you to do:"

"Back up, or let's think this through.   Don't just do what I tell you".

"Don't be afraid to ask questions for clarification of the request".

"Think through alternative solutions BEFORE acting upon it.   It's ok to discuss these with me.   I will not think any less of you".

"Believe in your knowledge and experience or the experience of others".

"Don't be afraid to ask for help."

"What's important is a good quality decision, not just a quick resolution."

What happens otherwise is that the Hispanic employee is so eager to please his "master", that very little thought goes into the resolution.   The Hispanic employee just wants to get it done quickly fearing retribution, etc.   This can result in costly mistakes, re-works, misunderstanding, rising costs, conflict, etc.

Here's the Six-Step Problem Solving Model:

Step 1:   **Define the Problem**
              Definir el Problema

Step 2:   **Analyze Potential Causes**
              Analízar Causas Potenciales

Step 3:   **Generate Alternatives**
              Generar Alternativos

Step 4:   **Select Best Solution**
              Selcciónar Mejor Solución

Step 5:   **Action Plan**
              Plan de Acción

Step 6:   **Evaluation & Implementation**
              Evaluación y Implementación

Step 1:   **Define the Problem**
              Definir el Problema

Create Problem Statement:

(What specifically is the problem today, right now, etc?)

Examine any data, the nature or extent of the problem and the business relationship, objectives and priority within the enterprise. Use data to describe:

1. What and how the situation is currently:

2. How should the situation be? (Desired State)

What is the difference between the current situation and how the situation should be?

_____

4. What outcome do you want from the situation?

Questions to ask about the "gap" between what it is and what it should be:

Is the problem measurable "as is" terms? Don't try to knee-jerk solve it!
Is the "desired state" described in measurable terms?
Is the problem statement free of causes or solutions?
Is the problem statement supported by available data?
Is the problem sufficiently limited in scope for a solution to be actionable?
Is the problem within the group's control? Define exact boundaries of control for the Hispanic employee!
Is the problem related to achieving business objectives?
Have we assembled the right people or team to work on this problem?

Identify the Problem:

Gather ideas or information about the problem.
Collect data and other documentation such as production, sales, employees, customer surveys, feedback, reports, memos, etc.
Relate topics to objectives, business impact, and process.
Establish boundaries for problem solving.
This is an excellent time to gather ideas and opinions from Hispanic employees about the problem. This will be a

tremendous motivator. Hispanic employees will be hesitant at first, but will quickly adapt. The obvious and ultimate transition for you and your organization is to begin receiving ideas and opinions with having to ask.

Characteristics of Good Problem Statements:

Characteristic
Define specific symptoms. These must be: Specific Measurable Understandable
Do not imply the underlying causes to the problem. Stick with the symptoms.
Stay away from implying a solution, or "knee-jerk solution, or "quick-fix" solution.
Don't blame, crucify, or make example of anyone.

Sample Problem Statements:

- Unable to answer call by third ring
- Plan is not cost effective, 20 % more than anticipated.
- Staff is not adequately trained to meet demand
- Specific machines keep breaking down
- Low production: 60% of plan instead of projected 80%
- Long set-up time (symptoms: no output).
- Supervisor & operator frustration due to ill trained staff.
- Inventory or procurement costs are higher than expected
- Parts do not conform to blueprints and specifications
- Nonconforming parts: too much rework, 30% scrap

Examine the Data

Obtain additional data needed to narrow the problem.
Display data in various formats: charts, graphs, pie charts, logs, tables, etc.
Interpret and clarify the data from the various formats.
Compare data with the business and enterprise objectives. How does your department roll up into these goals and objectives?

Tools for Collecting, Analyzing & Displaying Data:

Checklists
Logs (log books)
Production sheets
Computerized reports
Interviewing
Surveys
Questionnaires

Tools for Generating Ideas:

Brainstorming

Documentation

Flow Charts
Graphs
Log books
Tables
Pie charts, etc.

Step 2: **Analyze Potential Causes**
Analízar Causas Potenciales

In this step, we're going to analyze potential causes and how they impact the different areas involved. You may want to write a brief summary of the existing problem and where you want to be after the problem has been resolved.

List potential causes
Identify probable causes
Identify and prioritize root causes

Turning data into information:

Random data ➡ Categorize ➡ Useful
Information

Prioritize
Find Root Causes
Weigh severity of Root Causes
Select Root causes to work on

Revise Problem Statement

Now don't be afraid of root cause analysis.
It's a big word for getting to the bottom
of the matter in a systematic way.
Below is a really simple illustration
to help you understand the process.

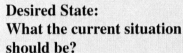

Desired State:
What the current situation
should be?

| Obvious Probable Cause | **Have the Hispanic employee**

"Why" and "what" in between each of the levels. |

| Obvious Probable Cause | *"Que" esta pasando*
"por que" esta pasando la situación? |

| Then, deeper and deeper discovery. |

Questions To Ask:

- Does the data analysis verify the problem statement?
- Are root causes supported by the data analysis?
- Is the problem statement still appropriate?
- What is the Impact to the customer, person, team, process, department, or company, etc?

Identify Probable Causes:

- List probable causes. Use the root cause chart on the previous page.
- Use other methods such as Ishikawa or fish bone analysis,
- Forcefield Analysis (We will not get this in-depth in this book. You may wish to purchase Total Quality Management TQM, or Total Production Management TPM curriculum)
- Apply criteria of action items that are within the scope of the individual or team.

Analyze Causes:

- Select probable causes for data collection.
- Design collection instrument(s), checklists, logbook, etc.
- Get consensus from the individual or team to collect data, analyze it, and display it.
- Identify root causes preventing the desired state. Forcefield analysis would be appropriate here.

Tools for Collecting, Analyzing and Displaying Data:

Cause & Effect analysis
Check lists

Cost-benefit analysis
Force-field analysis
Histograms
Interviewing
Pareto analysis
Pie charts
Surveys
Questionnaires
Flowcharts

Select Causes for Action:

Prioritize root causes.
Select root causes to work on.
Revise the problem statement if necessary.

Try brainstorming with Hispanic employees for generating ideas. This process will be new to most Hispanic employees, but it can be fun.

Motivator:

Asking for opinions or recognizing Hispanic employees for their contribution will create trust and motivate Hispanic employees to become more involved.

Guidelines for Brainstorming:

- Identify target cause or issue
- Solicit freewheeling ideas in a safe, nurturing environment.
- Set ground rules. Let people know that there are no "dumb ideas" anything and everything goes.
- No discussion of merits or judgement of potential of suggestions. What you want is to open the floodgates to

any and all potential solutions, no matter how "crazy" they may be. Who would have thought the wonder drug of the 20th century, penicillin would come from rotting fruit?

- Give a specific amount of time. Usually 5-10 minutes. Go three rounds at least in order to generate enough ideas and suggestions.
- Go for quantity, not quality at this point.
- Write down all ideas.
- Categorize the ideas & suggestions.
- Begin analyzing each branch of ideas for possibilities, then expand (piggybacking or hitchhiking) on the ideas until something crystallizes or synthesizes.

Synthesis:

Synthesis is a technique that combines two or more good ideas into one. This is where we get the word synergy, meaning that two people's combined actions or resources create a better product, relationship, strategic alliance, etc. than one alone.

Optional Ideas:

Round Robin -- The facilitator goes around the room asking each person for their ideas. Allow people to "pass" if they have no ideas. You may want to use this method as a precursor to the above freewheeling. It's more structured and formal appealing to the formality of the Hispanic culture.

Note Pad Method – You can use this method when the situation is sensitive. Just have each person write down their ideas on a piece of paper, fold it and turn it in. This method is very non-threatening, but leaves you with a large amount of responsibility. It may create doubt as to hidden agendas, and you're "stacking" the results.

Sticky Note Method – This method is similar to freewheeling and is extremely effective with the highly visual Hispanic culture. Basically, people write down as many ideas as possible on sticky notes in the allotted time. Then you post the notes on the wall for all to see. You then begin your process of categorizing the sticky notes, and then prioritizing towards the right next steps. One drawback may be that functionally illiterate people may not be able to write in either English or Spanish, so you may want to pair them up with someone that is able to write. This can slow down the process, but at least you have included everyone.

Step 3:   Generate Alternatives
**   Generar Alternativos**

This next step is the sensibility or reality check stage. It explores all of the options, asking the main question;
"Have we exhausted all ideas?

I tell Hispanic employees to come up with ideas for resolving the issue, then digging deeper to find the hidden treasure, el tesoro Escondido. People can understand this and get excited about the picture this paints. By now, many of you have figured out that I am an eternal optimist. This comes from a childhood of having to overcome adversities such as: being beat up in the first grade, the sixth grade and being jumped, along with four of my friends, in high school by a gang of 25.

Back to the subject: The problem needs to be reviewed in a non-judgmental way, listing all of the possible solutions.

Take a look at the macro view and reduce the list to a few potential options to come up with the best solution.

Review problem statement
Produce list of potential solutions
Fine tune potential solutions

**BEST
SOLUTION(S)**

Notice in our funnel illustration above, that I purposely did not say final or ultimate solution. This is something you MUST translate to Hispanic employees so that they can cope with continual change that is today's dynamic workplace. If you don't do this they will become cynical and you will lose trust.

Questions to ask:

Have we exhausted all ideas?
Have we avoided evaluation or judgements?
Have we thought "outside the box"?
Have we looked for ideas from individuals outside our immediate workgroup, department, division, etc.?
Is there a common understanding and agreement about the suggested solutions?

You can gather ideas from within the group or outside the group using:

Interviews- This works well in getting input from employees within or outside the group. It's especially effective in creating intradepartmental communications because people begin communicating more. It's also a nice break from the job for some folks. Make sure you monitor this process, but give Hispanic employee's breathing room. Also, don't insult or offend people by asking them to do this during their break. This information gathering becomes an integral part of their job responsibilities.

Coach the Hispanic employee and discuss what questions to ask, or what the big picture might look like at the end of the information gathering process. Make sure Hispanic employees understand the purpose behind this process and that it's not punishment or an exercise in futility. Help them understand especially that good, solid decisions take time.

Motivator:

This creates more trust, independence, and understanding of other functions or departments within the organization. A big "win" is increased intradepartmental communications, and a person's understanding of why "quick decisions" aren't made.
Encourage Hispanic employees to utilize this same process in their personal lives to get to the next level of excellence and position in life. Stress how important it is for them to teach these methods to their children.

Now you have become an integral agent of change within the Hispanic community. Doing your part in helping to break some very destructive and antiquated cultural shackles.

You will not offend, when you say it in a manner that people understand your good intentions.

Tools for Producing Alternative Ideas:

Brainstorming
Mind Maps – Putting the problem statement at the center of the paper, then major causes as radials out from the center. Each of these radials can be broken down into even more details
Nominal Group Reduction
KT Evaluation – What's causing the problem: man, machine, method or process, material, environment?
SWOT Analysis – Strengths, Weaknesses, Opportunities, Threats
Divergent Thinking – If the answer is obvious, look at the not so obvious
Convergent Thinking – Consists of narrowing down the immense number of possibilities into a smaller, more manageable number. Come up with alternative or plan "a", or contingency plan "b", "c", etc.
have Assumptive Reversals
Evaluation by Analogy -- this type of idea generation searches for a similar problem within or outside the organization to discover how it was solved. Once that is found out then one proceeds to solve it the same way. I call this looking at other's "best practices".
Heuristics – Heuristics provides aid or direction in the solution of a problem, it explores the problem solving techniques, education, skill or experience that finds a solution without checking all of the alternatives. This process utilizes self-educating techniques (such as evaluation of feedback) to improve performance.
Dominance Method – This method puts a list of criteria on the horizontal axis of a matrix and alternatives on the vertical axis. You then proceed to cross out alternatives if they do not meet the specific criteria, or you can put "yes or no" and go with the solution that features the most "yes's". (See below)

	Options Fix	Buy New	Sub-contract	Re-work	Re-train
Criteria ↓					
Time	N	N	N	N	N
Cost	Y	N	Y	Y	Y
Production	Y	N	Y	N	Y
Competi-tiveness	N	Y	N	Y	Y

The "Ben Franklin" -- A very similar method is the "Ben Franklin" where you create two columns. Place all of the reason in favor of the decision on one side and all of the reasons against on the other. You make a decision based on which side outweighs the other.

Additive Weighing – This method is designed to select one best solution based on the ranking of the alternatives. I.e.: ranking 1-5, 1-10, with 1 being the most important. Any zeros would get thrown out.

Cost-Benefit Analysis – Evaluates, especially with financial transactions, where the parties look at payback period, break-even, return on investment, etc.

Morphological Analysis – This method forces connections between different types of alternatives.

Step 1: List important problem attributes or traits.
Step 2: List as many features as possible under each trait.
Step 3: Complete your feature list, then make different combinations of features. See following example:

Problem	Problem	Problem	Problem

Trait	Trait	Trait	Trait
Feature 1	Feature 1	Feature 1	Feature 1
Feature 2	Feature 2	Feature 2	Feature 2
Feature 3	Feature 3	Feature 3	Feature 3

You would be taking the best practices from feature 1, first column, feature 2, second column, feature 3, third column, etc.

Beware of Idea Killers:

It's a shame to go through all of this and then be shot down by what I call the "business prevention squad". These are the negative people in your organization that will tell you why your ideas won't work. You may hear some of these questions or statements:

- We're not ready for that yet.
- You're ahead of your time.
- That's not our problem.
- It isn't in the budget.
- Top management will never ok that.
- Let's shelve it for the time being.
- Has anyone ever tried this before?
- It won't work in our industry.
- Will you guarantee it will work?
- But we would also have to change the…
- Let's study the problem a little closer.
- It's against company policy.
- The supplier will never do that.

- The customer doesn't want (or accept) that.
- Since when have you become the expert?
- Why change if it's not broken?
- We've never done that before.
- That's beyond our responsibility.
- Get these people involved? Don't be ridiculous!
- It won't work, we tried that before.
- It costs too much.

Step 4:   Select Best Solution
**   Selcciónar Mejor Solución**

Step four helps Hispanic employees determine the selection criteria. In the beginning you may want to select a best solution using consensus, or exploring divergent ideas. This methodology encourages individuals or groups to come up with new ways of looking at a problem.

Focus on many ideas, generating as many ideas as possible.
If the answer is obvious, encourage not so obvious solutions or contrary solutions. Encourage a devil's advocate (abogado del diablo) to help you find "hidden treasure".

Convergent thinking narrows down the possibilities into smaller, more manageable factors. One alternative may be enough, and then implement a contingency plan.

Things to consider:

Time: short term, medium-term, and long term...
Time: How much time can the organization dedicate to the matter at hand given other priorities?
Cost
Resources needed, and amount of control

Utilizing Criteria in Order to Select the Best Solution:

Eliminate or combine ideas
Design an instrument or tool to facilitate your selection
Use customized forms to keep track of variables and/or data
Checklist
Control list
Establish consensus as to specific process and completion attainability
Get feedback from all team members, owners, or stakeholders

Tools for Gathering, Analyzing & Displaying the Data:

Control List
Cost-Benefit Analysis
Forcefield Analysis

Effort-Impact Analysis – Good method for stop and go decisions that DO NOT involve money...

Label the benefit axis in terms of impact, savings, improvements, etc.

Label the cost axis in terms of effort, time, level of work required, etc.

Develop action plan, selecting the best alternative based on the criteria:

Effort-Impact Analysis:

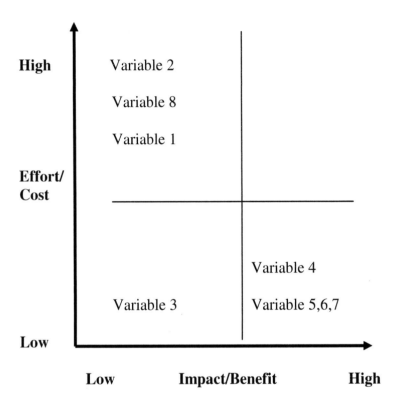

You can plot the different variables from a list you create and plot them in the respective quadrants in order to help you select the best decision.

I.e.: Variable 3 = Low Effort/Low Impact/Low Cost, Variable 4 - 7 = High Benefit/Low Cost/Low Effort, Variables 1, 2 & 8 = High Effort/High Cost/Low Impact.

Tools for Documenting Process and Action Planning:

You may want to display your findings using...
Flow charts
Gantt Charts
PERT Charts

Step 5:   Action Plan
Plan de Acción

Problem solving and planning can take as little as a few minutes, or it can take several months. What's important is figuring out what tasks must be accomplished or completed, and attaching a time-line to it. It's a good rule of thumb to differentiate in advance, if the solution is a process or a project.

Project:

A series of tasks occurring once.   Example, building a bridge.

Process:

An activity that occurs repeatedly.   An assembly line or fulfilling a merchandise order.

Write a detailed plan listing the action steps, roles and responsibilities of all interested parties, start times, end times, estimated time (minutes/hours) to complete and costs.
Develop an action plan to reach the Desired State. Determine whether you will start at the Current State and move forward, or whether you will start at the Desired State and work backwards.

Divide the solution into parts. Delegate assignments as necessary. Here's where you will need to assist the Hispanic employee know who to delegate to and how to communicate effectively and collaboratively. Only one person or department should be in charge of any given task. Exceptions might include the person doesn't have the necessary skill-set, cannot see it all the way through to completion for some reason, or are separated geographically. Here's were diversity works for you, as task sharing works best when each person provides a different skill, level of experience or contribution in order to succeed.

Set sub-goals or milestones. This portion is critical in motivating the Hispanic employee. Effective follow-through is critical until the skill level and trust is up to, or close to, the self-reliant level.

Have approvals centralized and minimized. Multiple approvals create confusion and bottlenecks, causing ineffective project management. (Minimize "red-tape"). One sure way to minimize bureaucracy is to get pre-approval from the next level(s) above as to who should have approval authority or ownership.

Work the most difficult, most important milestones first.

Fill in the necessary tasks between each milestone.

Make sure supporting areas know what they are providing:

- Information
- Money
- Equipment
- People
- Space, etc.

Sometimes support means having a "champion" within the organization who will provide you with the clout, or political backing necessary for you or your Hispanic employees to complete the project or process. Determine the timeline utilizing Gantt charts, roles and responsibility Deliverables charts, critical path charts, etc.

Know whom you need to keep informed about progress on a regular basis. Add up the costs.

Sample Responsibility Chart

Task or Decision Deliverable	Person Responsible	Date Due	Right Next Step (RNS)

Sample Gantt chart: Inviting employees to Quarterly State-of-the-Company Meeting

Objective: 1Q Meeting		TIME (Days/Weeks/Months)				
Task	Person(s) or Dept. Owner	3/15	3/22	3/29	4/6	4/13
Set Date	All					△

Task	Who						
Select Site	All	△					
Organize /Collect/ Prioritize Data	Luis - MIS	△——△					
Decide on Data	ALL		△——△				
Create Power Point Slides	Linda-Admin.		△——△				
Select Presenters	All	△					
Practice	Project Mgr./Presenters		△————————△				
Invite Employees	Linda-Admin.		△——△				
Set-up breakdown	Eddy-Maint.	△——△	△			△——△	
Evaluate Debrief	All						

Step 6: **Evaluation & Implementation**
Evaluación e Implementación

You'll notice in the GANTT chart above that the last task to complete was evaluation and debriefing. This is an often-overlooked critical component to continuous improvement. Many times debriefing consists of water-cooler talks amongst a few employees when it needs to be a formal feedback session of all interested parties.

Let me bring something to your attention here that this process is actually:

Evaluation  **Implementation**

Evaluation

First, you evaluate all of your potential alternatives and then decide on the best solution(s). This includes implementation planning. Don't forget about keeping subcontracting the task or activity as an implementation option also.

Second, after thorough evaluation, decide on an implementation strategy.

Third, evaluate continually making the necessary corrections throughout the process or project, including each milestone.

In the above example, the evaluation needs to incorporate a feedback mechanism from attendees. Don't just rely on feedback from the organizers. Be prepared for both positive and challenging feedback. This is the way positive change is created. Otherwise the same poor results tend to get repeated. You will need to coax feedback from Hispanic employees at first, until it becomes part of the routine.

Breakdown the event into components. You might want to start with the original tasks. Why reinvent the wheel?
Conduct the debriefing session in a non-threatening atmosphere.

- Avoid negative criticism and finger pointing.
- Concentrate on the process, instead of on the individual.
- Generate a list of possible alternatives.
- Decide on likely high-value remedies for next time.
- Create a dynamic policy and procedures manual so you can build continually on "best practices". Select "best practices" – Ask yourself what went really well?

Finally, you may want to utilize the International Benchmarking Clearinghouse (IBC) service of the American Productivity and Quality Center (APQC) for ideas on best practices and benchmarks in similar or other industries. The IBC is an organization for networking among businesses. The mission of the clearinghouse is to be a networking organization, a repository of benchmarking information in other organizations, and a center of expertise for benchmarking know-how. Although it is located in the United States it is international in scope.

Chapter 11

How To Motivate and Reward Hispanic Employees

This entire book has featured many different ways to motivate Hispanic employees. As a bonus, I want to give you some additional quick "tips" at-a-glance, to assist you in transforming the Hispanic employees in your organization into "world-class" employees:

Tip #1: Do Not Stereotype

Do not stereotype Hispanics as less intelligent than other races. If you do you will limit yourself from promoting capable Hispanic employees into jobs, such as engineering or computer programming.

High-technology companies have tended to make less progress in racial diversity, but have better track records on gender diversity.

Tip #2: Do not Embarrass, or Belittle. Create a Win-Win Strategy!

I know, some of you may be saying this goes with out saying, but I can't tell you the number of times I see this happening in the workplace, by both men and women!
It's important for the "macho" Hispanic male to "save face" with his colleagues. So, take the associate out of the situation or workplace immediately. It's as simple as saying, Excuse me, Carlos, would you mind coming to the office with me? I want to run something past you.

At this point it's important to involve this individual, and get him or her on your side. This is especially important if this person also happens to have tenure and is looked upon for direction by other Hispanic employees. When you present your "pitch" to his colleagues you don't want to guess whether he's in your corner. You want to make sure you have solid commitment. Lean forward while maintaining direct eye contact when you have come to an agreement. This move is highly primal: If you don't do this, or back away when you make your agreement, then it will be seen as a sign of weakness. You will then be undermined, or sabotaged behind your back. Keep your voice steady. Don't fidget!

Discuss your roles and responsibilities ahead of time, and have this individual participate equally with you. Present the change or policy together to the group. The other Hispanic employees will look at you, then at him, if both of you have agreed in advance on your strategy, then your stress level will be greatly reduced.

Tip #3: Women: Dress Colorfully Conservatively

It is essential that you maintain your decorum as a woman. Hispanic men appreciate and celebrate the differences in gender, but can respect authority no matter the gender. Avoid frilly or low cut blouses. Bright colors are a plus, although not too flamboyant. Remember that Hispanics are visual and happy colors are celebrated. Ethnic patterns such, as batíque or Central American patterns are a plus. Avoid African patterns such as leopard, or zebra. Slacks and company logo-wear are a safe bet too.

Tip #4: Build on Relationships

Build relationships. Be fair and consistent. Be approachable while maintaining an attitude of service and professionalism. Go to bat for Hispanic employees, especially if there is a language or other barrier. Be real. Do what's morally right!

Tip #5: Succeed with Diversity

Build on past successes to further broaden your company's diversity profiles.　　　　Honestly assess the racial and gender biases that have stifled some groups while promoting others. Create a diverse and inclusive workplace.

Tip #6: Create a Company that is Attractive to Women and Minorities

Leaders at all levels of the company must understand how stereotypes impact peoples' perception of their own power in an organization and create an oppressive environment for some, especially Hispanics who may already feel oppressed or discriminated against.

The Labor Department predicts that by 2005, 85 percent of new workers entering the labor force will be women or minorities. Labor's estimate of workforce growth also suggests workers will be in short supply through 2010 due to the aging baby-boomers. Companies already attractive to women and minorities will have a recruiting edge, especially since the average Hispanic age is around 30.

Create programs such as Hispanic Clubs, women in management and other similar programs. Day care and transportation are other important issues to Hispanic employees.

Tip # 7: Create a Mentor Program

Get executive management's buy-in that existing minorities, including women need to be developed to the next level of excellence through mentoring. Download and multiply your existing intellectual knowledge.

Tip #8: Find creative ways to break the "Glass ceiling"

The glass ceiling is defined as the negative stereotypes of minorities, which limit their ascension into high-paying executive-level positions. It is a covert or overt discriminatory practice of how minorities are selected for career tracks and/or advancement. Finally, it is a perception of how other managers perceive their work, or how employees perceive them.

Look for positive and creative ways to get past this. Don't keep talking about it.

Do something about it! Enlist a "champion" to promote eligible individuals, especially if they are minorities. Take negotiation classes, which will provide you with a systematic approach to getting what you deserve. It's just like buying a car... Why do some people pay top dollar for a poorly equipped vehicle, while others are able to drive off with the same car, fully-loaded, with extended warranty, floor mats, trim package, etc? Because they know how to negotiate! A huge part of negotiation is asking the right questions – This is an area where you don't want to rely on instinct!

Tip #9: Establish strategic alliances within the organization.

If you watch the TV show Survivor, then you know how important these strategic alliances can become.

Establish partnering core values and a formal agreement with your strategic partner.

In his book the Art of Partnering, Edwin Rigsbee writes about success factors to creating successful relationships.

These are:

- Trust –Taking risk in order to build relationships
- Tolerance & Understanding – Accepting ideas regardless of whose idea it is.
- Caring & Commitment – The old adage applies, especially with Hispanic employees: people don't care how much you know until they're sure of how much you care. Don't be afraid to tap into your maternal "caring" instinct, in order to tap into the Hispanic "commitment & loyalty" value.
- Synergy & Mutuality – Leverage the Hispanic employees' talents. Help them overcome the negative conflict habits by helping them realize that one and one equal three: she, he, and they. The "they" takes on a new stronger life, while allowing people to maintain their uniqueness and individuality.

Rigsbee goes on to map six steps to Partnering:

Step 1: Monitor

Study your business, and yourself. Observe, and identify areas of improvement.
Do a SWOT analysis on yourself and come up with a strategy to shore-up those weaknesses or bad habits that can become threats.

Step 2: Educate

Remember that your success is critical dealing with a population that needs the education to the next level of success. Continually educate yourself, and lead with this example.

Step 3: Select

This is another critical step, as all of your future efforts will be built on this foundation. Select partnering, whom to partner, knowledge-share, etc. Remember to select someone who matches your core values, attitudes, norms and objectives.

Step 4: Organize

The blending of the minds, talents, and efforts needs to be well organized in order to orchestrate a cohesive plan that ensures achievement of mutual goals and objectives. Communication. Phasing in the partnering relationship might be a preferred strategy in order to give the partners some time to "get acquainted". This can assist in the identification of milestones, or assessment points before moving the relationship forward. You may want to devise an evaluation form of some sort to measure progress, or to see how well the partnership is going.

Step 5: Charter

This is a formal written agreement so all issues and agreements are still crystal clear six months later. Additionally, this agreement serves to establish and clarify roles and responsibilities.

Step 6: Post Agreement

Regularly review your alliance. Periodically sit down and evaluate whether the relationship should be upgraded, maintained, or downgraded. To continually improve your business and the quality of the partnering agreement, share information regularly.

Tip #10: Meet with the right people as soon as possible whenever things get out of control.

Whether it's management or your direct reports. You want to assemble and enlist the assistance of the right people during difficult times.

Tip #11: Thank Hispanic Employees

A survey conducted on Women's Wire, December 20, 2000 asked women managers the following:

How often should you thank your employees for the work they do?

Never
Rarely
Constantly

1,892 people responded:

3% think being the boss means not having to say thank you
12% have been known to give praise
85% use praise as a motivational tool

Tip #11: Think "Big Picture"

One of the biggest hindrances to a manager is "control-itis", or micro-managing, concentrating on too much detail, wasting time on matters relating to the every day, especially those nasty everyday "fires." Concentrate, instead on the "macro-view": strategic, enterprise, goals and objectives.

Much can be said about wanting to seem busy and productive. This overcompensating may be perceived as lack of confidence by Hispanic employees, and will feed or confirm their level of uncertainty or inadequacy.

Tip #13: Learn to Delegate Effectively

Delegation empowers Hispanic employees allowing them a modicum of freedom within specific guidelines or parameters that you can exclusively or mutually agree on. Delegation allows you to multiplex (running simultaneous or parallel projects) as well as multi-task (running the various stages of completion).

Additionally it's a great way to groom or grow your own talent to the next level of productivity and competence. How are your Hispanic employees going to grow and assume more responsibility if you don't allow them to have it?

Why we don't delegate:

- We like control-preferring to do it ourselves.
- No time: too many things going on at once, or a tight deadline.
- No time: You procrastinated, or planned poorly.
- Can't trust others or you think you don't have the right employee (talent).
- Others can't do it as well as you can.   OR...
- Someone knows how to do it better than you do and you don't want to be embarrassed.
- You can do it faster, because you have the experience.

What can you delegate?

- Just about everything - Delegate it!
- If someone can do it faster, better, less expensive – Delegate it!
- If it stretches the individual employee or contributes to their personal growth – Delegate it!

What can we NOT Delegate?

- Personal, confidential, classified, proprietary, top secret, etc. – Don't Delegate it!!
- Discipline – Don't Delegate it!!
- If you own it, or it's ultimately your responsibility– Don't Delegate it!!

Management isn't about doing all of the work yourself, or telling Hispanic employees everything they should do; it's about getting your team to make decisions for themselves and consider new ways of doing things, breaking many of the old cultural shackles.

One of the easiest ways to get Hispanic employees to make decisions for themselves is to teach effective ways to make meetings work. Management obviously has to understand and make accommodations for the time Hispanic employees will be away from their regular work duties or responsibilities, the results will far outweigh the time away from their work stations, whether its assembly or high tech. Try not to get stuck on the "production reports" or output early on. It's critical that you relay this to the Hispanic employee to eliminate the fear of retribution for not producing adequately which might accompany this new freedom or responsibility. Remember what experts say: For every one hour that we invest in training, developing, planning or meeting, we will save three hours on the implementation, results, amount of mistakes, reworks, etc.

**Remember the
1:3 Rule...**

Don't go overboard with meetings: I remember one mismanaged healthcare company I worked at where they had meetings to *plan* meetings. This of course was a huge waste of everyone's time and becomes an excuse to get out of work. Do not condone or tolerate this type of behavior. When you tally the cumulative salaries for meeting attendees, then meetings need to become more effective. Additionally, figure out the average time wasted on meetings at your organization. A typical work year is approximately 2000 hours. What percentage of your work year is your organization spending in meetings?

Traditional meetings have different purposes. These different categories need to be shared with Hispanic employees. Remember to teach the process:

Meetings can be used to communicate – Concentrating on Task, Maintenance, or singular roles.

Meetings can be used for problem solving – Use the six-step problem-solving process contained in this text often.

Show Hispanic employees how to conduct constructive meetings that get results. This includes having prepared agendas, taking minutes, and what to do with those minutes, clarifying and assigning action items, (project manage), and sharing leadership or roles and responsibilities.

If you don't do this it'll be like a child playing on a sports team for the first time. (I don't want to lose you here, because I'm talking about sports: My 11 year-old daughter plays on a girl's basketball team and when properly coached, the girls play like a machine. They've got consistent, aggressive defense and have begun to share more of the offensive techniques.

In the beginning, though, some looked like a deer in the headlights of a car, paralyzed, not knowing where to move or awkwardly handling the ball. After a few, short weeks; even previously, non-experienced girls started developing into very competent players.

I use this illustration, because many Hispanic employees have extremely limited education and work-related fundamentals. Culturally they are hard workers; it's your job to turn them into "smart, competent workers".

Conducting effective meetings is one of the fundamentals you will have to coach them through until they "get it".

There are different types of meetings:

- Decision- making- to analyze decision options.
- Motivation- rallies, sales meetings.
- Informational- state-of-the-company,
- Problem-solving- resolutions of issues and concerns.
- Planning- planning of future events, activities.
- Strategic- planning of strategic implementations.
- Training- in-house, off-site, or on-the-job classes,

I would not recommend power lunches with Hispanic employees, as culturally, meals and business do not mix.

Conclusion:

The Hispanic worker wave is growing by leaps and bounds.

These are potential future leaders we need to develop for our organizations. As we develop these individuals, we need to address areas of competency which due to lack of education, or work experience are deficient. We also need to recognize why Hispanic employees may have a problem in completing their assigned tasks.

Reasons include:

1. Employee doesn't know why.
2. Employee doesn't know how.
3. Employee doesn't know what.
4. Employee has lost their focus.
6. Employee thinks they have a better way that is not consistent with your policies.
6. They don't like your way.
7. They have other priorities or have difficulty prioritizing.
8. There is no reward.
8. Employee is rewarded for doing substandard work.
10. Employee is afraid to do the job.
11. Employee's mistakes are not punished.
12. Barriers exist that are beyond the employee's control, or are perceived as being outside of their control.
13. Employee can't or refuses to do the job.
14. Employee has personal problems.
15. The job is simply humanly impossible.

16.   The job is really a supervisory or management job.
17.   Co-workers sabotage the employee's performance. (Barbero syndrome)
18.   Correct performance is punished somewhere, somehow.
19.   The delegated tasks are not congruent with the requested specifications.
20.   Employee thinks they're doing a good job or don't realize it's not the job for which they were hired.

As you address each of these issues and concerns then you will be better equipped to assess the basic Hispanic employee developmental needs.

Additionally, you need to assess the processes that support the Hispanic employee and champion change within the organization to set up the Hispanic employees for success. In many cases this will take a lot of courage on your part in challenging the "status quo". Either champion this change yourself or go through someone else with the necessary clout that can champion this change within the organization.

As your organization becomes a continuous learning organization, and you are able to tie these concepts into the Hispanic employee's "family" life, then you will begin to see dramatic transformational changes.

Hispanic employees are survivors and hard workers: Fully tap into this innate ability to adapt, innovate, and create. In return, be prepared to model the behaviors that you want, share the knowledge and vision, while creating a firm foundation: a foundation of continuous learning and improvement. This will give the organization the confidence to look beyond the un-educated or under-educated Hispanic worker and help you reach new heights that might lie beyond existing resources and the existing corporate culture.

Vaya con Dios. God be with you.

Appendix A

ADA Review

As you review applications and resumes, here is a note about Equal Employment Opportunity (EEO) and Americans with Disabilities Act 1990 (ADA) requirements.

Every job description should include the minimum qualifications necessary to perform the job. The qualifications must be consistent with the law. These principles will keep your personnel decisions in compliance with the law:

All job qualifications must:

Be objective
Can the qualification be described in terms of observable facts?

Be Uniform in Application
Can the qualification be applied in the same way to <u>everyone</u> being interviewed and evaluated?

Be consistent in Effect
Does it consider minorities, women, and the disabled?

Have Job Relatedness
Are the job qualifications directly tied to the specifics of the job?

Personal Note:

As a customer at a restaurant in South Lake Tahoe, California, recently, I witnessed a very capable waitress serving patrons from her wheel chair.

I still marvel at how efficient she is and how well she balances the plates on her lap.
Way to go!

Americans with Disabilities Act 1990 – is a broad-based Federal law that states that a "qualified person with a disability is a person who, with or without reasonable accommodation, can perform the essential functions of the job."

Important definitions in the Americans with Disabilities Act

Interviewers should understand a number of key definitions in the Act – definitions of "disability", "qualified disabled individual", "essential functions of the job", "reasonable accommodation", and "direct threat to safety "," unique hardship, as outlined in the act.

"Disability" under ADA

Under the ADA a "disability" is defined as a physical or mental impairment that

(1) Substantially limits one or more of the major life activities of an individual.
(2) Having a record of such and impairment, or
(3) Being regarded as having impairment.

"Physical and Mental Impairments"

"A physical or mental impairment" is defined in the Act as:

Any physiological disorder or condition, cosmetic disfiguration or anatomical loss affecting one or more of the following body systems: Neurological, musculo-skeletal, special sense organs, respiratory including speech organs, cardiovascular, reproductive, digestive, genitourinary, hemic and lymphatic, skin and endocrine.

Any mental or psychological disorder such as mental retardation, organic brain syndrome, emotional or mental illness, and specific learning disabilities.

"Major Life Activities"

"Major Life Activities" under ADA mean functions such as caring for one's self, performing manual tasks, walking, seeing, hearing, speaking, breathing, learning, and working.

"Qualified Individual with a Disability"

ADA defines a "Qualified Individual with a Disability" as: (1) an individual with a disability who (2) satisfies the requisite skill, experience and education requirements of the employment position such individual holds or desires and who (3) with or without reasonable accommodation, (4)

can perform the essential functions of such position.
"Essential Functions of the Job"

The term "Essential Functions" means primary job duties that are intrinsic to the job. The term "essential functions" does not include the marginal or peripheral functions that are incidental to the performance of primary job functions.

The Equal Employment Opportunity Commission (EEOC) which has the discrimination charge processing responsibility for the Act says they will consider the employer's judgement of what those essential functions are as well as any written job descriptions.

"Reasonable Accommodation"

The law does not give specific definition of "reasonable accommodation" but rather provides a list of examples which follow:

Modifying devices, services or facilities or changing standards, criteria, practices, or procedures for the purpose of providing to a particular person with physical or mental impairment... the equal opportunity to participate effectively in a particular program, activity, job or other opportunity.

The term also includes:

Making existing facilities used by the employees readily accessible to and useable by individuals with disabilities.

Job restructuring, part-time or modified work schedules reassignment or modification of equipment devices, appropriate adjustment or modification of examinations and training materials. In the Hispanic community this includes accommodation for language or illiteracy. The provisions of qualified readers or interpreters and other similar accommodations.

"Direct Threat to Safety"

An employer's paternalistic concern for the disabled person's safety cannot be used to disqualify an otherwise qualified individual. An employer may insist that an individual shall not pose a direct threat to the health and safety of other individuals in the workplace. Section 103(b). But the employer, if challenged, must be able to demonstrate a reasonable probability of significant risk or substantial harm

In determining significant risk the employer must consider four factors:

The duration of the risk.
The nature and severity of the potential harm.
The likelihood that the potential will occur, and
The imminence of the potential harm

A determination of whether an individual poses a "direct threat" should be made on a case by case basis with the above objective principles in mind.

Undue hardship – Types of Accommodation NOT Required

Employees are not required to make accommodations that are not "reasonable" or which would cause the employer "undue hardship". Any action that requires significant difficulty or expense, an action that is unduly costly, expensive, substantial, disruptive or that will fundamentally alter the nature of the program.

In the event of complaints under this section, the EEOC will consider the nature and cost of the needed action, the size of the employer, the overall financial resources of the total company, the number of persons employed at the facility, the effect, and the relation of the facility to the business as a whole, to determine whether undue hardship exists.

Experience of many companies with "reasonable accommodation" under provisions of the Rehabilitation Act of 1973 indicate that most accommodations can be installed at the cost of several hundred dollars and a few cases of "undue hardship' have been encountered.

Who is NOT Covered under ADA?

The Act includes a number of conditions that are disqualified from coverage and therefore are not "protected".

Active drug users (although rehabilitated drug users and persons who were incorrectly designated as drug users are covered).

Transvestitism, trans-sexualism, voyeurism, pedophilia, exhibitionism and gender identity disorders.

Appendix B

Bilingual Glossary

I remember conducting a twenty-week continuous improvement program at a place called Southern California Bindery and Mailing Services. For those not familiar with bindery services, some of these include folding, collating newspaper inserts, stitching, stapling, trimming, perfect binding of books, magazines and periodicals, attaching mailing labels via jet ink machine and the rental of mailing lists.

The work is hard, and the environment noisy. Most of the people working there are Hispanic, many were functionally illiterate, but most could read and write at least at the fourth to sixth grade level.

Most of the workers spoke limited English or Spanish only, creating a communication barrier. About three weeks into the program a couple of the workers including the production manager came up with the idea to create a bilingual glossary that would assist both the English and the Spanish-speaking employees avoid misunderstandings when it came to terminology used at the premises. It worked great! Conflict and frustration between employees dropped dramatically, mistakes dropped and both productivity and quality increased! As an added bonus both the English and the Spanish-speaking employees began to learn the terms in the other language, so the tool served as a bridge for both sides.

With this in mind I have compiled some basic terms which you will find helpful in order to assist you in creating bridges with your Spanish-speaking Hispanic Employees.

English	**Spanish**
Accountability	Contabilidad
Accounting	Department de Contabilidad
Analysis	Analises
Annual	Anual
Assemble	Ensemblar
Assignment	Tarrea
Boss	Jefe (Male), Jefa (Female)
Cause	Causa
Cause and Effect	Causa y Efecto
Check (evaluation)	Revisar
Check (monetary)	Checque
Client/Customer	Cliente
Customer Service	Servicio para el Cliente
Consensus	Consenso
Collaborate	Colaborar
Cooperate	Coperar
Cross-functional	Cruz funciónal
Cross-train	Cruz entrenar
Cross-training (ed)	Cruz entrenado
Department	Departamento
Easy	Facil
Engineer	Ingeniero
Engineering	Ingenieria
Error	Error

English	**Spanish**
Evaluate	Evaluar
Facilitate	Facilitar
Facilitator	Facilitador
Self-Directed Team	Equipo Dirigido por Si Mismo
Service	Servicio
Task	Tarrea
Task Group	Equipo de tarreas especificas
Expenses	Gastos
Goal	Meta
Impact	Impacto
Income	Ingresos
Income Statement	Cuenta de Ingresos
Invoice	Factura
Just in Time (JIT)	Fabricación al Tiempo
Lean Manufacturing	Fabricación Magra
Loss	Perdída
Mistake	Error
Objective	Objetivo
President	Presidente
Problem	Problema
P&L Statement	Cuenta de Gananzas y Perdídas
Proposal	Propuesto
Qualities (Characteristics)	Cualidades
Quality	Calidad
Quality Control	Control de Calidad (QC)
(High Quality)	Alta calidad
(Low Quality)	Baja calidad
Quality Control	Control de Calidad

English	**Spanish**
Quarter	Trimestre (Cada tres meses)
Team	Equipo
Technology	Tecnólogia
Together	Juntos
Tool(s)	Herramienta
Training	Entrenamiento
Lead Person	Supervisor or Superintendiente
Sales	Ventas
Sales Representative	Vendedor
Self-directed Teams	Equipos Dirigidos por Si Mismo, or Equipos auto-dirigidos
Semi-annual	Semi anual , Cada seis meses,
Share	Compartir
Sponsor	Patrocinar
Support (Gaining it)	Apoyo
Support (Giving it)	Apoyar
Supervisor	Supervisor
Manager	Gerente
U.S. Born Hispanic	Pocho (slang)
Why	Por que
Work	Trabajo
Work (To Work)	Trabajar
Year	Año

I hope this helped you. Why not create your own bilingual terminology book for your place of business?

References

Barnes, Tony. Kaizen Strategies for Successful Leadership, London, U.K.: Financial Times/Pitman Publishing, 1996

Bean, Frank D., Trejo, Stephen J., Capps, Randy & Tyler, Michael. The Latino Middle Class: Myth, Reality and Potential, Claremont, CA: The Tomás Rivera Policy Institute

Bosrock, Mary Murray. Put your best Foot Forward Mexico/Canada, A Fearless Guide to Communication and Behavior/NAFTA, St. Paul, MN: International Education Systems, 1995

Daniels, Aubrey C. Bringing Out the Best in People, New York, NY: McGraw-Hill, Inc., 2000

Heller, Robert. Motivating People, New York: DK Publishing, 1998

Henderson, George. Cultural Diversity in the Workplace, Westport, CT: Praeger Publishers, 1994

Jenks, James, The Hiring Firing (And Everything in Between Personnel Forms Book) Round Lake Publishing Company, 1994

Keirsey, David. Leadership, Temperament and Talent, Del Mar, CA: Prometheus Nemesis Book Company, 1998

Lee, Michael.   Selling To Multicultural Home Buyers, Winchester, VA: Oakdale Press, 2000

Lee, Michael. Selling To Multicultural Real Estate Clients, Winchester, VA: Oakdale Press, 1999

McAlindon, Harold R.   Management Magic, Lombard, IL: Celebrating Excellence Publishing, 1992

Rigsbee, Edwin R. Art of Partnering, Dubuque, IA: Kendall/Hunt Publishing Company, 1994

Scholtes, Peter R. The Team Handbook, Madison, WI: Joiner & Associates, 1993

Sosa, Lionel. The Americano Dream, New York, NY: Dutton Group, 1998

Stevenson, Nancy.   10 Minute Guide To Motivating People, Indianapolis, IN: Macmillan USA, 2000

Websites:

www.census.gov
www.nald.ca/fulltext/context/pg17.html

Quick Order Form

⌨Email orders: <u>Orders@mculture.NET</u>
⌐Web orders: www.mculture.NET
⌦Fax orders: 805-494-8829
☎Telephone orders: Call 805-494-0378
Credit Cards OK: VISA, MASTERCARD, AMEX

▭Postal orders:
Multicultural Associates, Carlos Conejo,
1560 Fremont Drive, Thousand Oaks, CA 91362
USA.

Please send the following books, disks or Reports:

_____

_____

Please send more FREE information on:

Speaking/Seminars   Consulting
Mailing Lists   Books & Training Materials

Your Name:

_____

Address: _____

City: _____

State:_____ ZIP: _____

Credit Card Number: _____

Expiration Date: _____e-mail Address: _____

Sales Tax: Please add 8.25% for products shipped to
California Addresses.
Shipping and handling: U.S. $5 for the first book or disk.